· MARY JO SHARP ·

W H Y

DO YOU
BELIEVE
THAT?

· A FAITH CONVERSATION ·

LifeWay Press.
Nashville, Tennessee

Published by LifeWay Press®
© 2012 • Mary Jo Sharp
Reprinted 2015

Item 005513459
ISBN 978-1-4158-7415-8

Dewey decimal classification: 239
Subject headings: APOLOGETICS \ WITNESSING \ FAITH

To order additional copies of this resource, write to LifeWay Church Resources Customer Service; One LifeWay Plaza; Nashville, TN 37234-0113; fax 615.251.5933; phone 800.458.2772; email *orderentry@lifeway.com;* order online at *www.lifeway.com;* or visit the LifeWay Christian Store serving you.

Printed in the United States of America

Adult Ministry Publishing
LifeWay Church Resources
One LifeWay Plaza
Nashville, TN 37234-0152

DEDICATION

This study is dedicated to all those who have
asked me to support my beliefs over the years
and who privileged me with engaging conversations.
It is also for Amanda, Joseph, Roger, and Emily:
the "A Team" of love and encouragement!

ABOUT THE AUTHOR

Mary Jo Sharp is a former atheist from the Pacific Northwest who thought religion was for the weak-minded. She now holds a Masters in Christian Apologetics from Biola University and is the first woman to become a Certified Apologetics Instructor through the North American Mission Board of the Southern Baptist Convention. A clear communicator with a teacher's heart, Mary Jo finds great joy in discussing the deep truths of her Lord and Savior.

CONTENTS

INTRODUCTION

Welcome to *Why Do You Believe That? A Faith Conversation*. We live in a world desperately in need of truth and the Truth. Many have given up on knowing truth believing it to be relative and subjective. To make a clear case for God in our day represents a great challenge. Fortunately we not only represent a great Lord, but great challenges lead to great lives.

I want to strike a balance here between encouragement that you can do this and a realistic view of the challenge. Hosea 4:6 sounds like our day when it says God's people are "destroyed for lack of knowledge."

To make the case in our day requires work, but every great undertaking demands similar effort. This study purposes to help you to sharpen your conversation skills for that great task. Together we will work to equip ourselves as apologists—those always ready to give a defense to anyone who asks a reason for our hope and to do it with gentleness and respect (see 1 Pet. 3:15-16).

I want to thank you as we begin. You can do this. You can be a good representative of Christ in our day. Together, and I hope with aid of small group, we are going to undertake the sharpening of our conversation skills. If you do this work you will know more of what you believe and become better able to represent those beliefs in a winsome way to others.

Make no mistake about it, however, the obstacles exist. God's call will stretch your comfort zone. This is not the work for others with a certain gift or calling. It is the work of the body of Christ: to bring truth, which is light, to mankind. We cannot afford to view this work as a luxury; lives are at stake.

Here at the beginning please let me make some suggestions. First, you can read and study this member book on your own. However, if you will share it with at least one other believer or preferably with a small group, your gain will be multiplied. Second, you will see that this is a book. Reading only will net you slight benefit. Fill in the activities. We learn by actually doing. You will find encouragements to take practical steps in conversations with others. Third, as suggested above, do the study together. Hold each other accountable. Encourage each other when the going is difficult. Talk together about the concepts you find difficult. Practice actually making the case.

Fourth, begin the lifelong journey of study being a representative of Christ entails. In these pages we have tried to balance training in the skill of good conversation with the actual content of those conversations—facts and arguments. Recognize that this is absolutely not a one-volume, all-you-can-know about apologetics. I have tried to give you some factual information you can use, but far more I have sought to help you develop the conversation skills you will need. If you come out better equipped to enter into conversation about God with those outside the faith, I will consider our goal achieved.

Fifth, we have produced video-teaching sessions for this study. They will make it easier to lead a group. Because we learn in more than one way, they will be helpful in reinforcing the study. Do not feel that you cannot do the study without the video, but I would encourage you to use all the tools available. In addition to the leader kit, you will find video session downloads and leader helps at *www.lifeway.com/maryjosharp*. I will also be seeking to support you in your quest through my Web site, *http://confidentchristianity.com*.

Finally I have supplied many suggestions for further study in the area of apologetics. You do not have to be an expert to represent truth in our day. The opposite is actually true. As you get into conversations, the needs will drive you to answer the questions you encounter.

Thank you again for caring enough to pick up this study. The stakes really could not be higher. The rewards could not be greater. May the challenging journey be a great adventure for you and life for many.

Mary J. Sharp

INTRODUCING APOLOGETICS

GROUP

Where were you born? What was your family like?

How long have you lived in your present home, and who shares it with you?

What difference do you think it would make in your life if you felt really comfortable sharing your faith with others?

What would you like to gain from participating in this study?

VIDEO GUIDE

Apologetics: to make a _____ or present a _____

1 Peter 3:15

Apologetics answers our _____ and gives us _____ _____ to believe in God.

Why do we do apologetics?

Reason 1: Apologetics is _____.

Reason 2: Apologetics helps you discuss your beliefs with _____.

Reason 3: Apologetics is the _____ of Jesus.

Reason 4: To spread the _____ message.

1

Imagine you are sitting around a family dinner table having some great conversation. You are discussing politics, the economy, the church, and other generally broad issues. One of your family members asks you about your church and how things are going there. You begin to discuss the latest activities, including last week's sermon on faith, when all of a sudden one of your family members says:

"Faith is a lack of critical thinking."[1]

What do you do? Do you balk at their comment? Do you quickly change the subject? Do you nervously laugh it off? Do you angrily accuse your family member of being an ignorant fool?

How do you think you might have responded if you had adequate time to think about your response?

Think of another scenario in which you are at work and a fellow employee approaches you with a book in hand entitled, *God Is Not Great.* You immediately notice the negatively charged title but aren't sure of the contents. This fellow worker is a dear friend with whom you have shared your faith but who did not make a decision to trust God. She drops off some paperwork, smiles, greets you, and then turns to go to her desk. What would you do?

What do you think you would have said and/ or done (notice: not what you would have liked to have done, but what you'd have actually done)? Share responses with your group this week.

Why do you think you would respond in that way?

Though the responses vary from person to person, talking with women around the country I find similar themes. Many women aren't discussing belief in God because they feel intimidated, inadequate, or insecure when it comes to this kind of dialogue. Some women are talking to people but their conversations seem fruitless or the conversation quickly gets shut down. Some women say they don't do well speaking to others because they themselves have a tendency to be defensive. Other women reveal they don't want to seem like they are "shoving their religion" on someone else.

Most of these women did not have similar issues when discussing nearly any other topic; the issues were almost exclusively related to discussion about belief in God. Though for some shyness may be a factor, generally women do not feel confident in discussing God. In this study, we are going to discover some confidence builders to help you have faith conversations anywhere, at any time.

• • • • •

DAY ONE

WHAT IS APOLOGETICS?

Joan Rivers used to say, "My mother could make anybody feel guilty—she used to get letters of apology from people she didn't even know."[2] Actually, an apology is a defense of a particular position. In a court of law, the defense lawyers present an apology for their client. They make use of evidence to build a case for their client's position. So an apology equals a defense or a case for something.

The word comes from the Greek in 1 Peter 3:15, "In your hearts honor Christ the Lord as holy, always being prepared to *make a defense* to anyone who asks you for a reason for the hope that is in you; yet do it with gentleness and respect" (emphasis added).

Peter told persecuted Christians not to fear those who were persecuting them but to:

1) trust God as holy (that is, really believe God knows what He is doing) and
2) be ready to tell anyone who asks (even the persecutors) why they have hope in God.

What change in your life, relationships, and self confidence do you think it would make for you to be better able to do those two things?

GREEK word: *apologia* = a defense

Modern understanding of an apology is asking for forgiveness. The ancient understanding of *apologia* was making a case or defending an idea.

Peter's words carry a strong message for us today. Not only are we to have an apologia ready to give to anyone, but we must be able to give it even in the face of persecution, with gentleness from God and respect for the person. The apostle Paul was a great

example of a man who was ready to give a defense of what he believed in any situation.

Contrast the two meanings of apology.

1) Modern understanding of an apology =

2) Ancient understanding of apologia =

We see examples of making a case in many places in Scripture. In Acts 17, Paul was walking through Athens on his way to speak in the synagogue when he noticed the idols all around him that were part of the culture of Athens. Deeply moved by the power of cultural influence on the people, he made a case for God utilizing the things he saw around him.

Paul gave a quick case against belief in the pagan gods of Athens and a quick case for belief in the resurrection of Jesus.

Identify one point Paul made against belief in the pagan gods and one point he made for belief in Jesus as you read Acts 17:16-32.

• **Against belief in pagan gods**

• **For belief in Jesus**

Paul made an apologia, an apology. He built a case for belief in God.

Think about a reflection of our culture you see or hear daily. Consider a billboard or radio commercial. Think of one way you, like Paul in Athens, could use this item as a springboard for conversation about belief in God. Plan to share this with your group this week.

To engage in apologetics, we can use everyday items from our culture to discuss the truth about God.

Write a definition of apologetics in your own words.

The word *apologia* is used 10 times in the New Testament. Particularly memorable is Acts 26:1-32 when Paul makes his case before King Agrippa. Paul laid out why he believed Jesus is the resurrected Son of God. When Festus claimed Paul was out of his mind, Paul replied, "I am not out of my mind, most excellent Festus, but I am speaking true and rational words. For the king knows about these things, and to him I speak boldly. For I am persuaded that none of these things has escaped his notice, for this has not been done in a corner" (vv. 25-26).

DAY TWO

WHY APOLOGETICS?

MY STORY

As a young minister's wife, I began doubting my faith in God. I think several factors played into this doubt.

First, I was a former atheist, raised to respect persons of all backgrounds, including religious backgrounds. I had been skeptical about and suspicious of religion, particularly Christianity. I thought religion was for "weird" people who were pretty well scammed into giving their money to a church in return for eternal rewards.

I hadn't spent much time studying my beliefs or Christian beliefs. Rather I reflected the influence of Hollywood and television toward a distrust of religion and religious people. If God was really like George Burns in the *Oh God* movies—a nice old man who popped in and out of people's lives to give advice—I didn't have much need for that kind of being.

I thought I was smart enough to figure life out on my own, and the corruption I saw from some high-profile church leaders troubled me. I certainly didn't want to be associated with the kind of dishonesty shown by TV preachers who claimed moral authority and then transgressed those very morals.

I came to faith as a result of a high school teacher I respected. He gave me a Bible and said when I had difficult questions about life, he hoped I would turn to the Bible. In college, after a couple of years of reading the Bible and going to church on my own, I became a Christian at the age of 20.

After becoming a Christian, I was disturbed by the notable disconnect between the people who professed the truth of God's Word and their lack of adherence to that truth. As a young minister's wife (and a young believer) I saw a lot of ugly things in the church: gossip, slander, false humility, authoritarianism, destructive jealousy, inflated egos, devastating moral failure, and more. I seemed to rarely encounter a person who felt responsible to live as though God's Word were actually true. They could preach it, discuss it, and sing about it, but living like it was true seemed to be out of reach. Worse yet, I found myself failing over and over. So I began to wonder if there was any such thing as a real believer in God.

During all this time, I was not cultivating a deep enough understanding of my faith to combat the hard questions about God I encountered. To the average person, I would have looked like a committed believer. I went to church every time the doors were open. I taught in the youth group. I helped my husband with both music and youth ministry. I was a counselor for church camp. When I wasn't teaching, I went to Sunday School and asked difficult questions. Yet, I wasn't really all that different on the inside, and I certainly wasn't discussing my belief in God with non-Christians on a regular basis.

I discussed some of the reasons for my doubt about God's existence. Name some reasons you have heard, both inside and outside the church, for why people doubt that God is real.

How do you react to those reasons?
○ **I have the same questions myself.**
○ **People who doubt God are just foolish.**
○ **I have faced my doubts and answered them with facts.**
○ **Sometimes I feel like I'm drowning in my doubts.**

ACCORDING TO Gary Habermas, professor of apologetics and philosophy at Liberty University, doubting God in some way is one of the "frequent and painful problems" plaguing Christians.[3]

For me all these factors came together to create the perfect storm for doubt. I began to ask why I believed in God and how I knew God was even real. During this time, I went looking for the answers to my questions about my faith.

I had stumbled into the field of apologetics. As I read arguments for and against belief in God, I began to see that belief in God was reasonable and well evidenced. It was not just based in feelings. I also began to see Jesus as a real person, who was really God, and who really had the solution to humanity's problem. I began to gain confidence that what I had believed about God was not just a fancy or a whim but was the actual truth about this life.

I began to realize that I, and we as Christians, needed to do three things. For ourselves we need to discover the real answers to our honest questions. We need to become sufficiently adept at handling the truth so we can feel confident, and we need to be about the job of sharing the truth.

YOU CAN remember these reasons for apologetics with the memory aid I call the ABCs.

ANSWER DOUBTS

BUILD CONFIDENCE

CHANGE LIVES

1) ANSWER DOUBTS

The study of apologetics can answer doubts and give us solid intellectual ground on which to stand.

EVEN COMMITTED CHRISTIANS
QUESTION THEIR FAITH AND
WONDER IF IT'S TRUE.[4]

In Luke 7 John the Baptist questioned his faith in Jesus. John had seen the miraculous appearance of the Holy Spirit at the baptism of Jesus, yet in prison John doubted so much he sent men to ask if Jesus was really the Messiah (see v. 20).

Jesus didn't rebuke John for asking this question. He didn't say, "John, you just need to have more faith." Instead, Jesus provided evidence of His identity. He made a case (a defense) to establish His identity by healing people.

We can make a case for belief in God to answer the doubts of believers. To have doubts is OK, but we need to take sufficient steps toward alleviating them. Christians who have grown up in the church may not have even begun to answer the questions that plague them. Yet, many go from a childhood acceptance of the facts of Christianity based on the confidence and trust in leaders (their parents, clergy, etc.) to a reexamination of how much of their early learning is their own belief.[5]

Do answering doubts and offering reasons for belief in God take away from faith in God?

Is stronger faith the answer to doubt? Why or why not?

The term *faith* has become somewhat convoluted in our current culture. It seems to mean something like believing what you know ain't so or believing something is true despite the evidence or lack of evidence. However, a faith not based on knowledge of God, including physical as well as supernatural evidence, is not the faith described in the Bible. Hebrews 11:6 states, "Without faith it is impossible to please him, for whoever would draw near to God must believe that he exists and that he rewards those who seek him."

What does the statement "a faith not based on knowledge of God, including physical as well as supernatural evidence, is not the faith described in the Bible" mean? Really think about it and write your own explanation.

Note the last two words in Hebrews 11:6: "seek him." What kind of activities can you do to seek Him, that is to build faith?

List actions you can take to acquire:
1. supernatural or spiritual evidence?

2. physical or historical evidence?

A person of faith has to first believe in the existence of God. How many people have a weak, anemic faith because they haven't feasted on the evidence? The passage of Scripture continues on to describe God's physical interactions with His creation. Theologian J. Gresham Machen said it this way:

FAITH IS INDEED INTELLECTUAL; IT INVOLVES AN APPREHENSION OF CERTAIN THINGS AS FACTS; AND VAIN IS THE MODERN EFFORT TO DIVORCE FAITH FROM KNOWLEDGE. BUT ALTHOUGH FAITH IS INTELLECTUAL, IT IS NOT ONLY INTELLECTUAL. YOU CANNOT HAVE FAITH WITHOUT HAVING KNOWLEDGE; BUT YOU WILL NOT HAVE FAITH IF YOU HAVE ONLY KNOWLEDGE.[6]

2) BUILD CONFIDENCE

Answering doubts or questions can build confidence. After I began to answer some of my most pressing questions, I discovered that Christianity had the best answers to my toughest questions. When I began comparing, I found that Christianity made the most sense as a worldview.

WORLDVIEW: the sum of our total beliefs about the world, the "big picture" that directs our daily decisions and actions[7]

When I began comparing other worldviews, I learned to ask how these systems of thought answer such questions as:
   1) How did the universe and creatures come into existence?
   2) Is there such a thing as good and evil?
   3) What is the problem of mankind?
   4) What is the solution to mankind's problems?

Once I realized I had the best answers to these questions through my belief in the Christian God, I became much less intimidated to talk to other people about what they believed. Through talking to others about their beliefs I found out that not a lot of people have studied what they believe and/or why they believe it.

3) CHANGE LIVES

Building confidence in what we believe can change lives—both ours and others. As I began to learn about my beliefs and discuss them with people of different backgrounds, I made a shocking discovery. I began to change in some aspects of my own personality. This was something I did not expect, that actually having to defend what I believed and why I believed it would change me from the inside out.

I think my daughter best expressed the change when she told me that I wasn't "petty" anymore. She said, "Mom, it seems like you've figured out what is important and what's not important."

Wow. My daughter was a preteen at the time and I didn't even know she knew what "petty" meant.

Dream a little. What would you like to see changed in your own life and personality?

How might building confidence in what you believe help to make that sort of change?

As we saw in Hebrews 11:6, to draw near to God, we must believe that He exists. To experience the fruit of faith, we have to get back to something as fundamental as believing in God's existence because: "People may not always live what they profess, but they will always live what they believe."[8]

I couldn't live out a belief in God that wasn't real to me. I had to find out why Jesus was worthy of my trust and confidence. So I studied apologetics, and now every time a sneaky suspicion rises in my mind that this might all be some grand hoax, I have a whole body of evidence to the contrary. Further, God began to change me as I made a public case for my belief in God. As I began to defend what I believed, I came to understand more clearly why I believed in God. I found myself forced to grow because I needed to answer the questions and challenges.

In the process I have seen more and more that my trust in God is well placed. This in turn has given me confidence to speak to others about beliefs. So the potential in studying apologetics doesn't just lie in the changes possible for the individual but for all those who come into contact with the individual.

I discussed why I attributed the changes in my life to apologetics. List the reasons or changes that make sense to you.

Have you ever thought that studying apologetics (defending our beliefs) could lead to transformation of your life? Why do you think apologetics can have such an impact on us?

DAY THREE

OBJECTIONS TO APOLOGETICS

Many of us carry around ideas that cause us to avoid apologetics. We'll cover some objections today.

OBJECTION #1: APOLOGETICS IS AGAINST THE TEACHINGS OF JESUS.

We may think that arguing goes against the teachings of Jesus and the other New Testament authors. We need to recognize that arguing can be defined in different ways.

> (1) Argue: to give reasons for or against something; reason <argue for a new policy> or to give evidence of; indicate <the facts argue his innocence>[9]

This kind of arguing does not necessitate a poor attitude or hostile spirit. Jesus, Paul, and Apollos used arguments to interact with other people.

How would you describe in one word what the apostle Paul was doing in the synagogue in Acts 17:1-4?

Notice here that Paul is not just presenting the good news. He actually reasoned with the Jews. As D.A. Carson explains:

> LUKE'S CLAIM THAT *HE REASONED WITH THEM* RATHER THAN MERELY "PREACHING AT THEM" IS UPHELD BY THE TWO-STEP ARGUMENT: FIRST, THAT ACCORDING TO THE SCRIPTURES, THE MESSIAH ... WOULD HAVE *TO SUFFER AND RISE FROM THE DEAD,* AND SECONDLY, THAT *JESUS* OF NAZARETH WAS IN FACT *THE CHRIST.*[10]

The Greek word used for reasoning is *dialegomai*. It means "to converse, discourse with one, argue, discuss."[11] To reason with others requires give and take in the conversation: questions and answers. People will react differently to the reasoning of our beliefs.

Different people received Paul's message in different ways. But this doesn't mean Paul, himself, was necessarily being argumentative. The authors of the New Testament do not condone being an argumentative person. Consider a second definition.

> (2) Argue: to express different opinions about something often angrily <that couple argues so incessantly it's a miracle they're still together>[12]

This definition is about quarrelsome persons, who argue destructively. In 2 Timothy 2:23-24, Paul tells Timothy that we are to avoid foolish, ignorant controversies that result in quarrels. He says we are to not be quarrelsome but kind to everyone. This passage is not about avoiding arguing for our beliefs with others.

The good news of Jesus is not a foolish, ignorant controversy, but it can result in quarrels. Remember the different reactions to Paul in Acts 17. A quarrelsome person will be mired in foolish controversies. If we read further in 2 Timothy 2:24-25, we'll see the purpose behind our kindness and gentleness is for the express purposes of teaching people, correcting opponents, and gaining knowledge of the truth:

THE LORD'S SERVANT MUST NOT BE QUARRELSOME BUT KIND TO EVERYONE, ABLE TO TEACH, PATIENTLY ENDURING EVIL, CORRECTING HIS OPPONENTS WITH GENTLENESS. GOD MAY PERHAPS GRANT THEM REPENTANCE LEADING TO A KNOWLEDGE OF THE TRUTH.

Paul's teaching applies here to a specific problem in Timothy's church in Ephesus. However, this same teaching can be applied to our interactions with both Christians and non-Christians. Think of one person you know who is not a Christian.

Make a commitment here to not engage in foolishness but to be kind and gentle with them even if you must "patiently endure evil" for the purpose of leading them toward truth.

Write your commitment in a sentence.

Now do the same for a person you know who is a Christian with whom you've had anger and quarrels.

Write your commitment in a sentence.

While we must be willing to argue the truth of our beliefs, we must never be foolishly quarrelsome.

Contrast two familiar meanings of argue:
1) argue = making a case using reasons

2) argue = heated, aggressive shouting match

Think of a time when you discussed your beliefs with a person and the conversation began to sour or become heated. Can you remember what sparked the anger?

What could you have done differently to avoid the rise of anger while still engaging in the discussion on beliefs?

For additional examples in Scripture, look to Jesus using reason and arguments in Matthew 22:23-32, Apollos refuting arguments in Acts 18:24-28, or Paul arguing persuasively in Acts 19:8.

OBJECTION #2: YOU CANNOT ARGUE PEOPLE INTO THE KINGDOM.

Agreed! Whew. I bet you thought I was going to argue with you on this one. I'm not. However, I'm going to go a bit further with this idea. Whenever I've heard this objection it has been coupled with a statement similar to "We just love people into the kingdom" or "I just give them Jesus." Though these statements may appear right on first reading, the statements have a problem.

We cannot love, argue, or "gospel-present" people into the kingdom of God. Why not?

As Greg Koukl, Christian apologist, states, *"You cannot love someone into the kingdom.* It can't be done. In fact, the simple gospel itself is not even adequate to do that job. How do I know? Because many people who were treated with sacrificial love and kindness by Christians never surrendered to the Savior. Many who have heard a clear explanation of God's gift in Christ never put their trust in him."[13]

That's because it takes the work of the Holy Spirit to bring a person to God: every time. When the Spirit is at work in any of these endeavors, then we may see a person come to trust Jesus as their Savior. John 16:8 tells us, "When [the Holy Spirit] comes, he will convict the world concerning sin and righteousness and judgment."

OBJECTION #3: I JUST NEED A SIMPLE, CHILDLIKE FAITH.

Over the years, I have encountered this objection to making a case for what we believe about Jesus. It seems to pit a childlike trust in God against an evidenced and reasoned trust in God. We need not do so. Let's read the passage from which this objection is often taken: Matthew 18:1-3.

What was the original question to which Jesus was responding?

What was the disciples' goal in asking Jesus this question?

What was Jesus' response to their question?

What character trait is Jesus emphasizing with His answer?

Jesus is not emphasizing intellectual simplicity when He uses the example of a child. He is emphasizing the humility of the child. Humility is an example of how we should view ourselves when we get a correct perspective on our relationship with God; rather than looking for our position in relation to other people. Further, though Jesus is not explicitly illustrating this point, we know that children have inquisitive attitudes interested in learning and discovering new things. So a childlike faith is more like a faith that is continually curious and seeking understanding about God. Paul taught about growing in the knowledge of God in Ephesians 4.

According to Ephesians 4:11-15, for what reason did God give prophets, evangelists, pastors, and teachers?

What does Paul say we are to no longer be?

What are we to grow up into?

Paul advises the church to continue to grow in their knowledge of God so that they are not fooled by cunning human arguments and so they are not like children in their faith. This same theme is found all over the Bible as the followers of God are encouraged to grow and mature in wisdom and knowledge.

What "cunning" human arguments can you think of that lead people away from biblical truth today? List some below.

Why is it so important to our faith that we do not remain as spiritual children but that we continuously grow in our knowledge?

Read Hebrews 5:11-14 and write a summary statement about the need to grow in our intellectual understanding of the faith.

In Matthew 18, Jesus claims that whoever humbles themselves like a child is the greatest in the kingdom of Heaven. If a person claims, in accordance with this passage to have a childlike faith, they are ironically claiming to be like those who are the greatest in Heaven. This seems to be a mistaken interpretation or misunderstanding of the context.

Do a quick review. List the three objections to apologetics we studied today and one way you can respond to each objection.

Objection #1:

Objection #2:

Objection #3:

DAY FOUR

MERITS OF APOLOGETICS

Yesterday we considered some objections to engaging in apologetics. Today we'll contrast the objections with the benefits or merits of such study. In a world where the media often trumpet claims by skeptics, best-selling books hawk atheism, and many university professors seem bent on destroying the beliefs of young Christians, it's increasingly important for us to articulate the reasons why our faith makes sense.

MERIT #1: HELPS CLEAR AWAY OBJECTIONS TO THE GOSPEL

Think back to the dinner scenario at the start of this week. Remember what the family member said ... that faith is a lack of critical thinking. It may be that this family member has an objection to faith in Christ that she needs help identifying and considering before she is ready to hear the good news of Jesus. I've had interactions with several people who came across negatively about or even hostile toward Christianity but who really just had one or two objections needing answers before they were ready to openly consider God's gift of salvation.

I remember a friend saying that he just couldn't believe in a God who judges sin. So I asked him to describe what kind of God he could believe in. Once he began to make a list of the characteristics he thought God should have, I saw that his list was strikingly similar to the Christian view of God; it was not like some mythological pagan God or some divine "force" (aka Star Wars). He thought God should be like the God I believe in. So I began to ask him to work out some details on each of those characteristics and how they would affect humans in this life. When we were finished I jokingly asked him why he wasn't a Christian already.

Think of an objection to Christianity you have heard lately, write it here, and note one question you could ask about that objection to further understand.

Each person we encounter will be at a different point in their thought process. How will we know where they are unless we find out and interact with their objections? Sometimes, the person with whom we interact will discover that they don't really object that greatly to God after all. Yet, it might take some patience as we peel back the layers of objections to find out what is the real issue.

MERIT #2: AIDS DISCOVERY OF AN EMOTIONAL HURT

Not everyone's objection is simply intellectual or even a reasoned argument. Some people have an emotional objection to God. They may have been hurt by a person or several people in the church. They may be struggling with difficult issues in this life that require more than just a polished argument.

C.S. Lewis, one of the most impacting Christian apologists in history, has well argued that God is the only answer to the problem of pain and suffering in this world (The Problem of Pain). However, after the death of his wife from cancer, Lewis struggled personally with doubt and depression and wrote about his emotional objections to God (A Grief Observed).

Why would a man who could argue rationally about the problem of pain and suffering still have problems with God when dealing with his own pain and suffering?

Lewis affirmed that he was not in danger of disbelief in God but of believing God to be malicious because of the depth of human suffering as he experienced it. In the Scriptures, Job also questioned God's character as did the psalmist for allowing suffering.

How can we help a person who has an emotional objection to God?

We can be there to work through problems with our fellow human. We don't have to be a listening ear after issues arise, we can take preventive measures as well. We can train ourselves and others in habits of the Christian faith (prayer, fellowship, discipleship) so that when our moods do greatly affect us, we will be able to rightly handle them with truth. This was also C.S. Lewis's solution in *Mere Christianity:*

THE FIRST STEP IS TO RECOGNISE THE FACT THAT YOUR MOODS CHANGE. THE NEXT IS TO MAKE SURE THAT, IF YOU HAVE ONCE ACCEPTED CHRISTIANITY, THEN SOME OF ITS MAIN DOCTRINES SHALL BE DELIBERATELY HELD BEFORE YOUR MIND FOR SOME TIME EVERY DAY. ... NEITHER THIS BELIEF NOR ANY OTHER WILL AUTOMATICALLY REMAIN ALIVE IN THE MIND.[14]

Apologetics can help us distinguish between the person who has an emotional objection and the person with an intellectual objection. Then we can take the correct steps toward helping them work it out.

For example, consider the "hypocrisy" objection: "the church is full of hypocrites." I nearly always find this objection in a person who has been hurt by members of a church. Once in awhile, though, I hear it from people who've never been in church but have obviously been greatly influenced by something they've seen or heard.

I regularly respond by saying that the world is full of hypocrites, and some of them go to church. I was a hypocrite before I believed in God. Even though I now try to avoid hypocrisy, I still ultimately fail. Hypocrisy is a human trait but not a trait of God.

MERIT #3: CULTIVATES AN ENVIRONMENT OF LEARNING

I never really learned what I believed until I purposefully engaged with people who challenged my beliefs from an opposing view. Why? I didn't see the need to defend my position. When most people around me agreed with my view, there was no imminent force driving me to find answers. Plus, doubt about God wasn't discussed much in church. For me, doubt crept into my life while I wasn't paying much attention to my thought life.

Why does doubt creep in when we don't cultivate our thought life?

We shouldn't need a crisis of doubt in order to learn to support our beliefs. Instead, we should begin to study the reasons for belief in God out of a love of truth. Read 1 Corinthians 13:4-6.

In verse 6, love does not rejoice in unrighteousness but love rejoices in:

Christians are called to be those who love what is true. We are to be those who rejoice when truth prevails. When we educate ourselves in the truth, we are making steps toward the triumph of truth in our lives as well as in the lives of others.

We can begin to use good arguments and reason with people who disagree with us. We will learn. Others will learn with us. Remember the old saying, "It's a win-win situation"? Well, in this case, it is!

List three merits of apologetics.

Merit #1:

Merit #2:

Merit #3:

Can you think of more reasons for studying apologetics? Plan to share them with your group this week.

If you've had a prior aversion toward making arguments for belief in God, I hope that you've seen a different side to arguing this week. Jude urges the believers to "contend earnestly" for the faith (Jude 1:3, NASB), Paul makes arguments for belief in God (see Acts 19:8), and Jesus thoughtfully and logically engages the religious thinkers of His day (see Matt. 22). The purpose behind apologetics is to help people with objections to the Christian faith, but ultimately it is to see them come to know Jesus as their Savior.

DAY FIVE

THE FINAL APOLOGETIC

All through this study, you will find that I ask you to argue for the kingdom of God. I will be challenging you to ask questions of others and hold them accountable for evidencing and reasoning their own views. So we had to come to an understanding of what constitutes good arguing and bad arguing.

List one Scripture that supports a model of good arguing.

What is the difference between good arguing and bad arguing?

I have encountered bad apologists for the Christian faith. They may make strong arguments but do so while failing to uphold a biblical ethic toward other believers as well as toward nonbelievers. So their lack of upholding truth in ethics fatally damages their arguments for God. Read John 17:20-23.

Jesus had been praying for the disciples with Him that night, but who is He praying for in this passage?

What is Jesus' prayer for these people?

What is the ultimate goal of His prayer for these people?

Christian apologist Francis Schaeffer called this passage the "final apologetic." He states, "What is the final apologetic? *'That they all may be one,* as thou, Father, art in me, and I in thee, that they also may be one in us; *that the world may believe that thou has sent me.'* This is the final apologetic. ... We cannot expect the world to believe that the Father sent the Son, that Jesus' claims are true, and that Christianity is true, unless the world sees some reality of the oneness of true Christians."[15]

Why is our demonstrated unity and our love for one another the final defense we can give for the truth of Jesus? Because Jesus says the world will judge whether or not He was sent by God based on how we treat one another. Schaeffer said he cringed at this teaching of Jesus, because he knew we honestly were not loving one another in a way that would represent Jesus' identity effectively to the world.

Think about how a nonbeliever would view your interaction with and words about other believers. Can you say that they would see the love of the God who sent Jesus into the world to save the world through your relationships?

As we learn to defend the truth of the ideas and teachings of the Christian faith, we will also learn about how a powerful defense begins with living like the Christian faith is true. This idea will remain a theme throughout our study.

Write out the "final apologetic" in your own words.

Studying apologetics is not going to be about just learning arguments to use in debate or how to refute the latest atheist book. It is about becoming the kind of person who is attractive to the person seeking truth. It is about following after the teachings of the Lord Jesus Christ. It is about following in the great tradition of the apostles, such as Paul. And as you will see, it is about discovering, uncovering, and sharing truth.

I'm excited that you've chosen to join me on this journey over the next few weeks. Since, we've already covered quite a bit over this past week, let's take some time to reflect on what we've learned.

Write one thing you discovered for each lesson this week.

Day 1:

Day 2:

Day 3:

Day 4:

Day 5:

KNOWING
YOUR
BELIEFS

GROUP

Not every conversation will be jolly, but engaging in conversation on truth brings real joy. Truth is an end in itself so knowing and discussing truth is part of the "good" life. Truth brings joy even when the discussion is not necessarily happy. Love "rejoices with the truth" (1 Cor. 13:6).

What item from your everyday experience did you identify that you could use as a springboard to talk about belief in God?

What reasons for doubt about God's existence have you heard?

What can you do differently in conversations to avoid anger while discussing beliefs?

Describe an objection to Christianity. What's one question you could ask about that objection that might lead to further understanding?

VIDEO GUIDE

Ask "Why do you believe that?" of _____.

Knowledge gives us a _____ _____ for our conversations.

Hold yourself accountable for _____ _____.

Areas of knowledge in which we should be confident:

1. _____ do I believe _____ God?

2. _____ do I believe _____ God?

Knowing what we individually believe about God is as foundational for having good faith conversations, as a good night's sleep is to driving a car. If you don't have the resources you need, you might find yourself in quite a wreck. Yet, not many people would think to list sleep as an essential element to driving a car.

Similarly, Christians don't often say that their own understanding of the Christian faith is an important factor in having good conversations about belief in God. We tend to stress the methods of evangelism, instead of stressing the importance of our own foundations for belief in God.

Why do you think knowing what you believe about God is essential to having good conversations with others about God?

When you train yourself in your own doctrines you are helping others learn about Christianity as well as yourself. How is it helpful to others when you learn about your own beliefs?

Throughout this week, we will look at some beliefs that are foundational to our faith conversations. Each day will center on building an apologetic (a case) for one basic belief in Jesus Christ. The goal is to begin using these basic beliefs in everyday conversations.

• • • • •

DAY ONE

JESUS IS THE ONLY WAY

KEY QUESTIONS:
Did Jesus say He was the only way to Heaven?
Is it intolerant to say there is only one way?

Immediately following the last supper, Jesus began a lengthy discussion with His disciples, knowing that the hour had come for His departure from this life. The passage begins in John 13.

What question does Thomas ask of Jesus in John 14:1-7?

What is Jesus' response (first half of v. 6)?

Jesus has just told the disciples that He is going to His "Father's house." The Greek word used here, *oikia,* specifically means the "dwelling" place.[1] So Jesus is referencing the dwelling place of God: Heaven. When asked how the disciples will get to Heaven, Jesus responds that He is the way. Notice, He mentioned no rituals, practices, or moral codes. Jesus specifically stated that the way to Heaven is found through Him. Then Jesus further emphasizes His point.

How does Jesus complete the thought in the second half of verse 6?

Keep reading in John 14:8-11. What request does Phillip ask of Jesus?

What is Jesus' response?

Jesus offers more support for His claim that He is the way to God: He equates Himself with God. He specifically states that whoever has seen Him has seen the Father. Then He offers proof for His claim by saying if a person cannot believe that He is one with God based on His words, then trust in the evidence of His miracles (works). This is similar to Jesus' interaction with John the Baptist from our lesson in week one (see Luke 7:18-22).

How does Jesus' claim affect His teaching on salvation?

How is this different from the teaching of other religious teachers?

Though Christians rely on the teachings and person of Jesus to support their view of only one way of salvation, some people believe that the Christians who hold to this view are intolerant people. Yet this is a mistaken understanding of both Christianity and the concept of tolerance.

How would you respond to the statement that for Christians to say that Jesus is the only way is intolerant?

How do you define *tolerance*?

Tolerance means the ability or willingness to abide, bear, or put up with something, in particular the existence of opinions or behavior with which you disagree. In our current society, the concept of tolerance has become very mixed up. It has come to mean that a person must be "accepting of all views."[2] Yet, the definition of tolerance suggests that we bear with persons who hold those views or opinions, not agree with their views or opinions.

Write a definition of tolerance, emphasizing that we endure patiently people who hold opinions with which we do not agree.

Share your definition with someone in your group or a friend. Practice stating and explaining the definition.

Christians can become confused by a culture that has twisted the meaning of tolerance. They may feel as if they are "shoving their religion" on a person for discussing their belief in God. We must remind others that real tolerance extends to the Christians as well as to everyone else. The Christian view of salvation is one that a society of "tolerance" should be tolerating, even if some do not agree with it!

How would you explain that the Christian view should be tolerated?

Let's take this one step further. According to Jesus Christ's teaching, Christians are to go beyond the societal view of tolerance to a much deeper love for their fellow man.

In Luke 6:27-31, Jesus says to
_____ your _____ and
to do _____ to those who
_____ you.

Do you find it is easy or difficult to do what Jesus requires? Why?

What does He say to do in verse 31?

Why is treating others how we want to be treated important when we have disagreements on religious beliefs?

Jesus went on, however, to build a case for dealing lovingly with our enemies. Read Luke 6:32-36.

What does Jesus say about only loving those who love you?

What does Jesus say about only doing good to those who do good to you?

When you love your enemies and do good expecting nothing in return, on whom are you modeling your behavior?

Is this the kind of love supported by the current view of tolerance in our culture? Does our culture teach that you must love all people and do good to them despite their opposing views? No. The cultural view of tolerance has no tolerance for those people who do not accept all ideas as equally true.

What does this mean: "The cultural view of tolerance has no tolerance for those people who do not accept all ideas as equally true"?

NOT EVERY PERSON with whom you talk will view Christianity as intolerant. So do not first assume that everyone who is not a Christian holds to this view. If someone does bring up this issue in conversation, then you should ask them at least two questions:

1) Why do they see Christianity as intolerant?

2) On what are they basing this view of Christianity?

These are great questions for our faith conversations.

How could you explain to a person who thinks you are intolerant that Christianity is actually a very tolerant religion?

The Christian virtue of tolerance exceedingly surpasses the cultural view. Jesus commands us to love in spite of our differences of views and opinions. Why would we settle for a worldly definition of tolerance after considering the depth of the Christian virtue? We should not.

Actual definition of tolerance:

TOLERANCE: the ability or willingness to permit something, in particular the existence of opinions or behavior that one does not necessarily agree with[3]

Cultural view of tolerance:

TOLERANCE: accepting all ideas and opinions as equally true

Christian doctrine, based on the teachings of Jesus, shows us only one path of salvation, through Jesus Christ. He is the way to Heaven. Christians are not intolerant due to their doctrine of salvation. The Christian view is based on the biblical text. That text also teaches us a Christian ethic of loving all people and doing good to them, even if you disagree with them or consider them an "enemy." Jesus leaves no room for a church that hates or persecutes people of other beliefs. Our ethic is to be one that surpasses the cultural expectation.

CONFIDENCE BUILDER: You may encounter a person who doesn't trust the church because of some of our history. As a representative of Christ, you need to acknowledge the truth that some people have taken irresponsible and destructive actions in the name of Jesus throughout history. If you have yet to study church history, it would be good to at least get the facts on some of the most frequently misconstrued aspects of church history.

Make it a point to learn something about (1) how Christianity originally spread to the world, (2) the church councils, (3) the Crusades, (4) the Spanish Inquisition, and (5) the witch hunts in colonial America. You also need to get some facts on the positive impact Christians have made on the world through building hospitals, shelters, and schools; distributing food, clothing, and water; and activism for human rights. What non-Christians may forget, or not know, is that atheism, Hinduism, Islam, animism, and other beliefs have had some of the bloodiest histories associated with their doctrines and teachings. We need to help people develop a balanced perspective on this issue.

RECOMMENDED RESOURCES: "Why God Allows Evil" by Dr. Clay Jones, audio CD lecture, available at *http://apps.biola.edu/apologetics-store/products/audios/item/why-god-allows-evil_CD; No Easy Answers: Finding Hope in Doubt, Failure, and Unanswered Prayer* by William Lane Craig; *The Problem of Pain* by C.S. Lewis; *That's Just Your Interpretation* by Paul Copan

DAY TWO

....

JESUS IS DIFFERENT IN
DIFFERENT RELIGIONS

....

2

KEY QUESTIONS:

Don't all religions teach basically the same
things?

Who is the real Jesus?

Does it really matter what you believe as long as
you believe?

Why can't all religious teachings be true?

On an episode of Oprah Winfrey's religious Internet course, "A New Earth," Oprah stated that the
purpose of Christ coming was not to die on the cross
for our sins but to show us the Christ-consciousness
that we all have within us.[4] She and her spiritual
guide, Eckhart Tolle, were teaching over two million
viewers that when Jesus says, "I am the way, the
truth, and the life," He meant that we all have this
quality within us. However, as we saw in our previous lesson, Jesus was not teaching this message
at all. Jesus was teaching on the way to Heaven.
Though we've only looked at one, we can see already
that Christianity does not teach the same basic
beliefs as Eckhart Tolle's new age spirituality.[5]

Christianity distinctly and exclusively teaches
that Jesus was God. Jesus calls Himself God using
a name that neither He, nor the biblical texts, ever
ascribes to anyone else. We'll look at a passage from
the Book of John to establish Jesus' self-proclaimed
identity. In our passage, a group of devout Jewish
people claim that Jesus' teachings and miracles
were demonic in origin. Jesus responds with a radical claim. Read John 8:48-59.

In verse 53 what does the group ask Jesus?

Write this question in your own words.

Jesus responds by saying that He doesn't glorify
Himself, but God glorifies Him. He states that Abraham saw His day and rejoiced. Of course, Abraham
died long ago. So the group asks Jesus another
question.

What do they ask (see v. 57)?

What is Jesus' response this time?

What does Jesus' response mean?

**Why do the people pick up stones to throw
at Him after His response?**

Jesus' response was quite radical if you think about
it. Jesus used the name of God spoken to Moses
in Exodus 3:14, "I AM." At the very least, Jesus is
claiming to be over two thousand years old (older
than Abraham). However, the reaction of the Jewish
people demonstrates that they understood Jesus was
claiming the very name of God to identify Himself.

In Christianity, Jesus claimed to be God. He's
not just one with God in some cosmic, impersonal
sense, as in the teachings of Oprah. He is the same
person as the Creator of the universe; as the only
God the Jewish people recognized. Do other religions
teach the same thing about Jesus? No.

Let's do a brief survey of a few other views about
Jesus as God.

ISLAM: Jesus is neither God nor God's Son. He is a great prophet, second only to Muhammad.

JUDAISM: Jesus is neither God nor God's Son. He is a false Messiah, possibly an unorthodox Jewish rabbi who was wrongly deified by the church.

HINDUISM: Jesus is one of many spiritual teachers or masters. He may be an avatar (manifestation) of the god Vishnu. As such, He would be one of many gods.

BUDDHISM: Jesus was just one of many enlightened ones. He was a Buddha-like figure for those in the West. Buddhists can accept Jesus as divine in the same way they may accept Buddha was divine.

HUMANISM: Atheist humanism denies God and usually sees no value in Jesus as a teacher; they possibly doubt His existence at all. Religious humanism sees Jesus as a teacher of good values and service to others but not as God.

MORMONISM: One of many spirit children created by Heavenly Father and Mother. The literal son of God in the flesh born by Mary (result of sexual union).

JEHOVAH'S WITNESS: A created being made by God. He was a perfect human; no more, no less.

NEW AGE MOVEMENT (Eckhart Tolle & others): Jesus was one of many great teachers but not the only God of the universe. Jesus realized His divinity and showed us that we could all realize our divinity.

Do any of these belief systems teach the same thing about Jesus as Christianity?

Write one major difference between the Christian view and one other view of Jesus.

Choose another view and write one difference.

Say out loud the two differences you just wrote; first to yourself, then later to someone in your group.

Why is it important to know that our basic beliefs differ from other religions and views when having faith conversations?

THROUGHOUT THIS STUDY, you will notice the attention I give to saying these statements out loud. The thoughts in our head usually sound very different to us once we try to verbalize them. It is important to practice saying out loud the kinds of statements we want to eventually say in conversations about faith; so we get used to how they sound. Practicing also helps us avoid two typical problems.
   1) Not knowing what to say
   2) Not saying what we
      intended to say

Hindu and native of India turned Christian apologist, Ravi Zacharias, says, "Anyone who claims that all religions are the same betrays not only an ignorance of all religions but also a caricatured view of even the best-known ones."[6] When we encounter the view that all religions teach the same thing we need to be gracious toward the person holding this view, gently correcting the error, realizing that we, ourselves, are still learning as well.

Write out one way that you could gently and briefly explain the major difference between the Christian view of Jesus and other views about Him.

Though we've discovered that religions don't all teach the same thing, there's more we need to address under this topic: Why does it matter if religions teach different things? Couldn't each one be true for whoever believes them?

How would you seek to clearly explain the problem with the idea that each view of Jesus could be true for those who believe the ideas?

CONFIDENCE BUILDER: If you are in a conversation with a person who thinks that all religions teach the same thing, you should ask the person: "How did you come to this conclusion?" Further ask for what the specific religions teach about God. Then you can interact with their answers. The person will hopefully begin to see that either they do not have the resources for making this claim or that the claim is false. In reference to the similarities among religions, G.K. Chesterton wrote, "The religions of the earth do *not* greatly differ in rites and forms; they do greatly differ in what they teach."[7] Chesterton further declares that pronouncing all religions as similar due to ceremonial aspects (priests, altars, feasts, rites, Scriptures, etc.) is "like alluding to the obvious connection between the two ceremonies of the sword: when it taps a man's shoulder, and when it cuts off his head. It is not at all similar for the man."[8] The teachings of each religion—especially about God, salvation, and man—are vastly different and have different implications for mankind.

In our current culture, we hear "to each his own," or "Whatever works for you is good for you, but whatever works for me is good for me." This approach even shows up with religious beliefs. It is called religious relativism. One problem with this view is that it is illogical to say that all religions are true when these religions/views directly contradict one another in their claims. To illustrate the point, we'll look at just one simple claim in two religions. For example, here are two claims about Jesus.

ISLAM: Jesus is not God.

CHRISTIANITY: Jesus is God.

What problem do I create if I say both of these are true?

Who is asking Peter and John this question?

What question was asked of Peter?

Let me give you a related, but imaginary example:
Imaginary-Church-of-Oprah: Jesus is Oprah Winfrey.
Christianity: Jesus is not Oprah Winfrey.

Do you see the problem now? Jesus cannot both be Oprah and not Oprah at the same time. That's illogical. The same is true with saying Jesus is God and Jesus is not God at the same time. It is illogical or absurd. Different religions make different claims about God and the path to God. Some of these claims directly contradict each other (such as on the person of Jesus and the nature of salvation).

What was Peter's response?

What is Peter's further response in verse 12?

How do Peter's words in this passage counter the idea that all religions are equally true for whoever believes them?

What is wrong with believing it is true that Jesus is God and that Jesus is not God at the same time?

Jesus and His disciples also believed not all religions had the truth about God. For example, we learned in day 1 that Jesus taught He was the only way to Heaven ... to God. In Acts, Peter also proclaims that Jesus is the only salvation, inferring that other beliefs are wrong on salvation. Read Acts 4:5-12.

Peter proclaimed that men can be saved through no other name than Jesus the Messiah. Peter's statement not only attributes the salvation of God to the person of Jesus, but it also contradicts the claim that all religions can be true, at least with regard to salvation. We must, however, remember that while we proclaim the truth we must also be careful to be respectful of others.

RELIGIOUS RELATIVISM "maintains that one religion can be true for one person or culture but not for another. No religion, therefore is universally or exclusively true."[9] If one view of God can be true for one person and another view of God can be true for another person, then it seems we could never know what is actually true about God. The resultant attitude is that we shouldn't try to push one truth about God.

You've probably seen Christians who have belittled someone on the basis of their beliefs. You may have heard the phrase, "hate the sin, but love the sinner." However, this is a difficult concept to translate to the world in a loving way.

How can you help convey an attitude of loving what is true and loving all people?

We can also see in the Acts passage that Peter equates Jesus with the one God of the universe; "there is no other name under heaven given among men by which we must be saved" (v. 12). No other worldview teaches that Jesus is the one God of the universe. To say that all religions teach the same thing about God is erroneous. To say that all religions are true for whoever believes them leads to accepting contradictory statements as true and proves to be illogical.

Why is it important to find out what is true about God?

How would you explain this importance to another person?

DAY THREE

JESUS' RESURRECTION IS FOUNDATIONAL TO CHRISTIANITY

KEY QUESTIONS:

Why is the resurrection of Jesus so important to Christianity?

Isn't the resurrection just a nice story, like other dying and rising gods?

How would you explain to a new believer the crucial nature of the resurrection of Jesus?

IF CHRIST HAS NOT BEEN RAISED, THEN OUR PROCLAMATION IS WITHOUT FOUNDATION, AND SO IS YOUR FAITH. 1 CORINTHIANS 15:14 (HCSB)

Some of the Corinthian Christians apparently did not believe in resurrection at all. Their disbelief is not unusual considering that Greek philosophy generally taught that the body was the prison of the soul, which was set free through death of the body. Paul penned 1 Corinthians 15 to teach some basics on the resurrection. Part of that teaching was the importance of the historical event. Read verses 12-15.

Paul says in verse 14 "If Christ has not been raised our preaching is _____ and so is your _____" (HCSB).

What does Paul mean when he says this?

In verse 15 what does Paul say that he and others would be guilty of for testifying that Christ was resurrected if He has not been resurrected?

Paul stressed the importance of the resurrection as the foundation for our faith. He emphasized that without this event we have no reason to put our faith in Jesus Christ. So Paul is attempting to root the resurrection firmly in history. He does not simply say it is a nice story by which we should live our lives. He says if no resurrection, then no reason for faith.

Paul further raises the stakes (as if they could be raised) by saying that not only is your faith useless without a resurrection, but you are also breaking one of the Ten Commandments by giving false testimony. Notice you are not just falsely testifying about any average person but about God Himself.

Write an explanation you could give to an interested unbeliever for your belief that the resurrection was an historical event.

CONFIDENCE BUILDER: Dr. Gary Habermas and Dr. Michael Licona have written a book building the case for the resurrection of Jesus as an historical event. They center their argument on four basic facts from the New Testament that nearly all scholars accept as historical: 1) Jesus died by Roman crucifixion, 2) Jesus' tomb was empty, 3) Jesus appeared to His disciples, and 4) Jesus appeared to skeptics and foes. Habermas and Licona look for various hypotheses to determine which one best explains all four facts concerning the death of Jesus and the subsequent events. The one that best explains all accepted historical facts is that Jesus rose from the dead. Their argument is "The Minimal Facts" approach.[10]

Paul doesn't stop by telling us that without the resurrection our faith is useless or that we are giving false testimony. He makes one more negative claim in verse 19. Read 1 Corinthians 15:19-20.

What does Paul say about those who believe in resurrection if there is no resurrection?

Why does Paul make this claim?

Given the cost of being a Christian in the Corinthian world, Paul claims, that without a resurrected Jesus, the Christians are the "most pathetic people on the earth."[11] "We are of all people most to be pitied" (v. 20). If there is no resurrection, then Christians have no hope for the afterlife, plus they have given up many "pleasures" of living for the moment in this life. Paul's argument here goes to its logical conclusion: no resurrection, no hope for Christians. However, Paul doesn't leave the argument there.

In verse 20, what does Paul say about the resurrection of Jesus?

Why would the resurrection of Jesus mean that God approved of His life (and message)?

What does "firstfruits" or "firstborn" of the resurrection mean?

When talking with others about your beliefs what can you tell them to emphasize the importance of an historically resurrected Jesus?

Christ being truly raised by God from the dead holds some huge implications for our lives and for our interaction with others. It means that we will live into an afterlife that includes a physical resurrection. Further, as Pastor Timothy Keller noted, "If Jesus rose from the dead, then you have to accept all he said; if he didn't rise from the dead, then why worry about any of what he said?"[12]

Jesus' resurrection gives His teaching power. It provides for Him God's stamp of approval on His life as vindicated through Jesus' defeat of death. This resurrection sets Jesus and His teachings apart from all other religious leaders.

"If Jesus rose from the dead, then you have to accept all he said." What are some of the things Jesus said that we must accept? (Hint: think back to day 1 of this week.)

In my conversations with people who don't believe in God (especially those raised in church), I often find that they presuppose my belief is that they should be doing everything Jesus taught. I've had to ask "Why would I expect you to obey Jesus' teachings if you're not a follower of Jesus?"

This one question actually opens up the conversation quite a bit. I don't expect unbelievers to follow Jesus' teachings. However, if a man who claimed to be God actually rose from the dead, I think it would be a bit foolish not to listen to Him; especially on His teachings about eternal life. Then if possible at that point, I move on to establish whether or not Jesus was resurrected. See the confidence builder for suggestions on what to discuss.

CONFIDENCE BUILDER: The most common argument I get in response to Jesus as actually resurrected is that many myths have gods who died and rose from the dead. So why should a person believe that Jesus' resurrection is real and these others are false?

First, this is not a very good argument at all: one thing looks like another, therefore neither is real.

Why wouldn't a person need to worry about any of Jesus' sayings if Jesus didn't rise from the dead?

That's just not good logic.

Second, there are not many dying-and-rising god stories, but there are a few.

Third, none of the dying-and-rising mythic gods are just like the resurrected Jesus. If the person making this claim reads the actual stories, they will find that the gods do not rise to a new physical life that is the model resurrection for all people. Most of the gods end up reigning in the land of the dead, returning to the underworld for part of the year or never rising from the dead at all; and none of their stories take place at a specific time in history, like Jesus' resurrection.

So major differences separate the resurrection of Jesus Christ from the dying-and-rising god myths. For more information on addressing this argument, you can read chapter 10, "Does the Story of Jesus Mimic Pagan Mystery Stories?" in *Come Let Us Reason: New Essays in Christian Apologetics.*

THE REASON THE RESURRECTION IS SO IMPORTANT TO THE CASE FOR CHRISTIANITY IS THAT … IT CONFIRMS THE TEACHING OF JESUS AS HAVING THE AUTHORITY OF GOD.[13]

The resurrection of Jesus is the foundation of our Christian beliefs. It is crucial to our faith that we know what we believe about the resurrection and that we can aptly communicate that belief with others.

DAY FOUR

JESUS USES GOOD REASONING

KEY QUESTIONS:

Why should we use good reasoning? Shouldn't we just learn the Scriptures?

What are some of the problems created when we don't use good reasoning?

Throughout my years in church, I have noticed a lack of emphasis on learning to reason well. We devote time to study what the Word of God says, but we don't spend time to understand the great arguments made in the Bible. Atheist groups such as the Freedom From Religion Foundation suggest that reason and faith are not even compatible. However, good reasoning is not in opposition to faith. Jesus Himself used good reasoning and held others accountable for poor reasoning.

JESUS DEMONSTRATED THE TRUTH OF HIS MESSAGE AND HIS IDENTITY OVER AND OVER AGAIN USING NEARLY EVERY METHOD AT HIS DISPOSAL, INCLUDING MIRACLE, PROPHECY, GODLY STYLE OF LIFE, AUTHORITATIVE TEACHING *AND* REASONED ARGUMENTATION.[14]

What question does the group of Sadducees in Matthew 22:23-28 ask Jesus?

What problem with their question do you see in verse 23?

Why were they really asking this question?

They approached Jesus not seeking truth but seeking to further a presupposition. They built their argument on the denial of a resurrection.

What two reasons does Jesus give for why their reasoning was faulty? (See v. 29.)

In verses 31-33 what argument does Jesus make to refute the Sadducees' false notion?

The Sadducees are a group of Jewish religious teachers who were well informed on the Scriptures. However, Jesus tells them that they did not know the Scriptures, which is why the Sadducees' problem about the resurrection arose. Wait a second. These are the well educated and studied Jewish religious teachers. As the *Bible Knowledge Commentary* states, "of all people certainly they should have known God's Word and His power."[15] But apparently, though they knew the Scriptures, they were still wrong.

In verse 30 Jesus actually gives the answer to their original question. What is His answer?

However, Jesus does not stop after answering their question. He pointed out that their reasoning was flawed because though they knew the Scriptures they had a false understanding of the afterlife. Verses 31-32 provide a prime example of how Jesus used good argumentation and reasoning. He doesn't simply answer the question: "You are wrong." Instead, He understands the Sadducees' theology and uses their theology to make a solid argument against their view.

The Sadducees don't believe in the resurrection, as noted previously, but they also accept only the first five books of the Bible as authoritative (the Torah). So, Jesus reasons with them from their own trusted Scriptures to show that there is a resurrection, since God proclaims Himself as a God of the living and not of the dead, as from His quotation of Exodus 3:6.

Do you see how Matthew 22:31-33 particularly demonstrates that Jesus used reason and argumentation? How would you explain the point to a friend?

Why should we take the time to reason with others?

When someone you hear misquotes and/or takes biblical passages out of context do you typically show them their error?

When I speak at conferences, I meet people who have family members that have either left the faith or doubt their belief in God. Many times, they tell me this person "knows their Bible" even better than they do themselves. We saw in our passage today that the Sadducees also knew their Scriptures, yet they were still wrong.

How can we help our family members and friends who "know their Bible" but are having troubles with certain concepts, like resurrection, Hell, or with doubt?

How does good reasoning and good argumentation help us to counsel others?

CONFIDENCE BUILDER: If God is "truth," as we are taught in the Scripture (John 14:6), then we should desire as much truth as possible so we can better know God. This means we must use the reasoning abilities given to us by God to discover what is true. Sincere belief in something is not enough; the belief must be true in order to get us to a better understanding of God. In his book, *Know Why You Believe*, Paul Little says, "Belief doesn't create truth. Unbelief doesn't destroy truth. Christian faith goes *beyond* reason but not *against* reason."[16] Though God will surpass our ability to reason about Him, He does not go against the reasoning ability with which He has endowed mankind. We must cultivate good reasoning as part of our love of the Lord God. You can begin with a basic book on detecting bad reasoning such as *The Fallacy Detective: Thirty-Eight Lessons in Bad Reasoning* by Hans and Nathaniel Bluedorn, written for preteens through adults.

What are some of the problems created when we lack good reasoning?

The Book of Proverbs says: "Blessed is the one who finds wisdom, and the one who gets understanding, for the gain from her is better than gain from silver and her profit better than gold" (3:13-14). As we saw with the Sadducees, failing to use good reasoning to

carefully think about our beliefs and the Scriptures can lead us to erroneous beliefs. It can also contribute to believers who hold a shallow Christianity; who don't know much about their faith. The resultant poor witness speaks ill of the gospel message. It gives the impression the message is not worth understanding the reasoning behind it.

How might poor arguments with bad reasoning adversely affect our listeners?

Inattention to our reasoning ability also speaks poorly of our Lord. Jesus was the greatest teacher who ever lived. Should we not be committed to a lifelong education to learn from Him and grow deeper in knowledge as His disciples (students)? We should. It is contradictory to tell the world Jesus, as the greatest teacher, has the most important knowledge a person can ever learn, while exemplifying a lifestyle lacking a desire to learn. This contradiction is fairly easy to spot by persons from inside or outside the church.

Why is it contradictory to say Jesus is the greatest teacher who ever lived while not having a commitment to our own education through discipleship?

Poor reasoning and bad argumentation between believers in the church also causes disunity and strife. When was the last time you saw a person's argument in a church meeting gently and patiently broken down to make sure it was well argued and coherent as part of loving God? Good reasoning helps us to keep our emotions in check and helps avoid destructive arguing, which certainly brings glory to God. We'll discover some basic areas in the next two weeks to help us begin reasoning well with others.

The main problem created, though, when we are not attentive to developing our thinking skills is that it goes against the greatest commandment.

What did Jesus say is the greatest commandment (see Matt. 22:34-40)?

We are to love God with everything He has given us. No part is to be left out. That includes our minds, which we must purposefully continue to develop as part of our love of God.

> IF WE ARE GOING TO BE WISE, SPIRITUAL PEOPLE PREPARED TO MEET THE CRISES OF OUR AGE, WE MUST BE A STUDYING, LEARNING COMMUNITY THAT VALUES THE LIFE OF THE MIND.[17]

DAY FIVE

JESUS' STORY HAS BEEN RELIABLY TRANSMITTED

KEY QUESTIONS:

Do we have now what they wrote then?

What is the importance of knowing the content of the original text?

Dr. Bart Ehrman, New Testament textual critic and best-seller author, has become popular in the media for his claim that we cannot know what the New Testament authors wrote. He says that it doesn't make sense to discuss things such as inspiration when we don't have access to what was supposedly originally inspired. He says all we have are copies of copies of copies of copies that are sometimes centuries later than the originals were written.[18]

However, Ehrman is not accurate in his remarks. The New Testament has been reliably transmitted over the last two thousand years; so much so that Greek scholar Daniel Wallace calls the evidence "an embarrassment of riches."[19] Let's briefly look at how we can know what the originals said. To see if what we have now is what they wrote back then, we are going to look at the bibliographical evidence.

BIBLIOGRAPHY is the study of books as tangible objects.

This field of study:

1) examines the texts of which books are made
2) studies the manner in which these materials are put together
3) seeks book's place and mode of origin
4) traces what happened to the books after their origin
5) is concerned with the relation of one book to another: the question of which manuscript was copied from which, which individual copies of printed books are to be grouped together as forming an edition, and what is the relation of edition to edition.

45

Bibliographical evidence answers questions such as:
- Was the document composed close to the time of the event(s) it describes?
- How many copies of the document are available to make a comparison?

Why might we need to establish the case for the reliability of Scripture before we can claim the inspiration of its contents when speaking with non-Christians?

CONFIDENCE BUILDER: Christians may be utilizing the passage from 2 Timothy 3:16, "All Scripture is breathed out by God and profitable for teaching, for reproof, for correction, and for training in righteousness, that the man of God may be competent, equipped for every good work" as an argument for the reliability of the Scriptures. However, this is a circular argument (a logical fallacy). We cannot effectively argue that the Bible is a reliable text because the Bible says it is a reliable text. The reliability of the text depends on the accurate transmission of the text. We must first establish that the writings we have today are what the authors originally wrote for a conversation on their inspiration to be fruitful. Otherwise, anyone could make a claim that a text is the inspired Word of God or God-breathed.

The authors of the thoroughly documented book, *Reinventing Jesus* sum it up with this statement:

THE NEW TESTAMENT MANUSCRIPTS STAND CLOSER TO THE ORIGINAL AND ARE MORE PLENTIFUL THAN VIRTUALLY ANY OTHER ANCIENT LITERATURE. THE NEW TESTAMENT IS FAR AND AWAY THE BEST-ATTESTED WORK OF GREEK OR LATIN LITERATURE IN THE ANCIENT WORLD.[20]

We know that the story of Jesus didn't change over two thousand years of copying it down because we have so many copies from so many different places all over the world to check it. How many copies of biblical manuscripts are there? For the New Testament we have:
- 5,700 Greek manuscripts
- 10,000 Latin manuscripts
- Plus Coptic, Syriac, and other Middle-eastern & European languages

The numbers will most likely only increase in years to come.[21]

If a scribe made a mistake while copying a biblical text in one location, say in Constantinople, researchers have thousands of other copies from Egypt, Syria, Italy, and all over the ancient world to cross-reference that individual copy. Unbelievable amounts of painstaking study have gone into comparing all of these manuscripts to determine the most reliable and best-attested readings.

So I could look at his copy and discern the error made. I could also trace all subsequent copies that transmitted his original error throughout the years by checking these in the same manner. Therefore, despite Bart Ehrman's concern that we have lost the content of the originals due to the copies of copies of copies, all those copies have helped to confirm the content of the original writings of the New Testament rather than in any way reduce their reliability.

If a scribe made an error in copying, how would we be able to detect his error?

Why is it beneficial to us today to have many copies of the New Testament texts?

What would you say to a person who told you that we don't know the content of the original New Testament texts?

For comparison, look at numbers of surviving copies of other ancient manuscripts.[22]
- Homer's *Iliad*: 1,757
- Writings of Herodotus, the "father of history": 83
- Plato's *Tetralogies*: 210
- Tacitus, the greatest ancient Roman historian (also a contemporary of Jesus), *Annals* and *Histories*: 31

This is quite a difference just in the numbers of surviving copies to check for accuracy between other trusted ancient texts and the New Testament text.

Since so many copies of the New Testament exist, we can be reasonably certain that the story of Jesus we have today is the same story the original authors wrote. So when we share the gospel message, we can have confidence that this message is based on the original written stories of Jesus Christ.

Why is it important to our conversations with others that the story of Jesus we share is the same as the originally written story of Jesus?

FOR MORE STUDY of the reliability of the New Testament manuscripts, check out the work of Daniel Wallace at The Center for the Study of the New Testament Manuscripts: *http://csntm.org*. A great introduction to the arguments for reliability can be found in his collaborative book, *Reinventing Jesus: How Contemporary Skeptics Miss the Real Jesus and Mislead Popular Culture*. Daniel Wallace also posts his debates with Bart Ehrman on New Testament reliability on the Internet. Search for "Wallace versus Ehrman."

How can you utilize this knowledge when conversing with others about your faith in God?

What could you say if a person says you cannot trust the Bible since it was written so many years ago?

Practice saying out loud what you just wrote. Perhaps have a family member or Bible study member ask you a question about the reliability of the New Testament.

Pray that God will put someone in your path who needs an answer in one of these areas.

Now that you have gained some knowledge in a few areas of Christian doctrines, let's review this week's key points.

Write the major point for each day of this week.

Day 1:

Day 2:

Day 3:

Day 4:

Day 5:

· WEEK THREE ·

LISTENING TO OTHERS

GROUP

When we know what we believe and why we believe it, we build confidence in our beliefs. That confidence helps us to better express our beliefs and helps us to better engage with people of different beliefs.

Why is knowing what you believe about God essential to having good conversations with others about God?

How would you respond to others who claim that to say Jesus is the only way is intolerant?

How could you explain to an interested unbeliever how you discovered why you believe the resurrection is an historical fact?

How would you respond to a person who said many myths have gods who died and rose from the dead?

What would you say to a person who told you that we don't know the content of the original New Testament texts?

VIDEO GUIDE

Reasons to develop listening skills:

1. What the _____ teach

2. What we know of _____ _____

_____ to listen

People are valuable for who they are; they are not _____

3. What we might be _____

First steps to listening:

1. Write the things people do when you are talking that _____ _____.

2. Assess how many of these things you've been _____ of.

3. Begin listening better by using the _____ _____.

Last week, we learned some basic arguments to defend our belief in Jesus. This week we are going to focus on one of the most important aspects of our faith conversations: listening.

From my experience, one of the main problems with our faith conversations is poor listening ability. We don't hear what others are trying to say nor are we listening for comprehension and understanding. If we don't listen well, our arguments for God may be ineffective as we lose the trust of the person with whom we are conversing.

We need to learn, or relearn, how to listen with love and respect before we can enter into conversation. Perhaps you are a great listener and this week will put into words what you already know to do so you can pass this skill along to others. Just like every area of our faith conversation, though, listening takes learning and practice.

This week we will break listening down into purposes as well as its practice.

. . . . .

DAY 1

LISTENING TO MINISTER

KEY POINT: Listening is loving people.

Though I'd like to start this week by saying that I've completely changed how I engage with people in terms of listening, I cannot. The truth is I'm not the best listener. I tend to break in while other people are talking. I often take what a person has said and relate it back to something about me. Worse yet, sometimes I don't actually hear a person because I'm thinking of what to say next.

How well to do you listen to others? Place a check mark to rate yourself as a listener.

|..|
1   5
POOR   BEST
LISTENER   LISTENER

Now rate yourself on the chart specifically for a situation in which someone is questioning your belief in God.

Did your number change? Why or why not?

It may seem odd to include listening in a study on apologetics. But as we grow in knowledge of our beliefs, the temptation may also grow to "give" others at least some morsel of our knowledge every time we're with people. Even after years of ministry, I must remind myself of what the Bible tells me about listening. Read James 1:19-20.

We are to be quick to _____.

We are to be slow to _____.

We are also to be slow to _____.

Why does James say to do these things?

Though this passage may seem like a good ol' super-familiar phrase, this is the point at which I see would-be defenders of the faith break down. They do not listen to the argument against their position. They speak too quickly and let their emotions take over. As James says, these actions never produce the righteousness of God.

Have you had troubles with allowing other people to speak while you patiently listen without interrupting?

If you have troubles with a spirit of argumentativeness or of impatience with others, ask God to help. Write a request or commitment.

Have you had troubles with another person who doesn't allow you to finish speaking before interrupting? What could you say or do to gently let them know?

Listening is such an important aspect of our faith that it could be called a "ministry" or service of the Christian faith.

THE MINISTRY OF LISTENING

Dietrich Bonhoeffer, brilliant Christian thinker and an outspoken opponent of the Nazi regime in Germany, described listening as the "first service" one owes to another. "So often Christians, especially preachers, think that their only service is always to have to 'offer' something when they are together with other people. They forget that listening can be a greater service than speaking. Many people seek a sympathetic ear and do not find it among the Christians, because these Christians are talking even when they should be listening."[1]

Why do some Christians (maybe even you and me) feel that we have to offer something every time we are with other people?

A few years ago, my husband and I attended a forum at New Orleans Baptist Theological Seminary. Part of the forum included the presentation of papers by some of the leading Christian scholars in the country. Following a paper presented by physicist Frank Tipler, an atheist audience member attempted to express his concern with a concept in the presentation. Immediately several young students began to answer his initial thoughts before allowing him to finish his point. He quickly became agitated. When an opportunity presented itself to interrupt, I asked the gentleman, "What are you trying to say that you can't seem to get out? We won't interrupt you anymore." Once he said his whole thought, his temper had noticeably changed.

Why did the atheist gentleman become agitated?

What would have been a better initial approach to the atheist's comments?

Have you been involved in a situation where someone became frustrated because they couldn't seem to finish their thoughts before being interrupted? If so, what was that like?

Jesus is not just concerned with making a right argument; He is concerned for the person. True concern, or love, for the person will involve discovering truth together, but it will not do so in a manner that is rude and belligerent. Read 1 Corinthians 13:4-5.

List the attributes of love described.

How can you apply these principles of love in conversations about belief in God with those who hold to a different view?

Listening to others is part of loving them. The reason we want to share our belief in God with others is out of love for them. We want others to discover the truth we have discovered in God. However, we must be patient with them, realizing God is the One who does the work; in His time, not ours.

If you do not love others, it will become obvious through your attitude and actions. Let's finish today with a time of reflection. Take time to allow God to search your heart.

Evaluate yourself on the two parts of this question: Do I really love other people?

1. How does the way I am willing to share my faith show I love people?

2. How does my willingness to listen show that I love people?

Take a few minutes to pray about this area of love. Ask God to bring to your mind how you already show love to others who are opposed to your view of God. Note your thoughts.

Ask Him to bring to your mind where you need to improve and note your thoughts.

DAY TWO

....

LISTENING TO BE ACCOUNTABLE

....

KEY POINT: Listening to others helps us check our thoughts against the thoughts of other people.

DO YOU SEE A MAN WHO IS WISE IN HIS OWN EYES? THERE IS MORE HOPE FOR A FOOL THAN FOR HIM.
PROVERBS 26:12

In a passage from Proverbs 26, Solomon discusses the nature of the foolish person. He utilizes some fairly striking imagery. Read Proverbs 26:1-11.

What is the overall picture painted by Solomon of "the fool"?

Name a few of the metaphors he used to describe the fool.

What does the metaphor "like a dog that returns to his vomit" mean in verse 11?

Solomon's description of the fool is extremely derogatory. It is a person that no one would ever hope to become. The fool is injurious to others (vv. 1-2), doesn't respond to intellectual appeal—only

to physical discipline (v. 3), is untrustworthy with messages (v. 6), is not worthy of honor (v. 8), isn't employable (v. 10), and doesn't learn from past mistakes (v. 11). However, Solomon is not setting up the image of the fool merely to describe the foolish person, he is going to make a shocking statement.

What does Solomon say in verse 12?

Describe in your own words what Solomon is saying.

It always stuns me when I meet a person who seems to believe that they have everything figured out. They won't take correction or even slight criticism. They are unapproachable and have no accountability for their beliefs. Solomon says this pride is more damaging to a person than is the foolishness of the fool. Solomon's warnings throughout Proverbs are just a small part of the overall warnings in the Bible to constantly seek wisdom through correction and instruction; not allowing pride to creep in.

We must take a position of humility of knowledge in this life realizing we can never "know it all." One way to encourage humility of knowledge is to really listen to others' ideas and thoughts.

How does listening to another's thoughts on a matter help us keep our thoughts in check?

How does listening to another's thoughts on a matter help keep our pride in check?

Even if you disagree with a person, what are some things you can learn from your interaction with them?

When we engage people in conversation we should always see this engagement as an opportunity to learn. We must constantly be mindful of the error of being wise in our own eyes. Our minds, and therefore our thoughts, are subject to the fallen nature of man. We should not expect that everything we are thinking is accurate all the time. To do so is an egregious mistake. To avoid this error, Solomon has some more cautions for us. Read Proverbs 12:15; 18:1-2.

Contrast the way of the fool and the wise in Proverbs 12:15.

Describe one instance in which you disagreed with a person's view, but you learned something from them. What did you learn?

AT THIS POINT, you might wonder if we should listen to everyone, even if they have different beliefs. I know I've heard church sayings like, "Ninety-nine percent truth and 1 percent lie is still a lie." While this euphemism may have come from a good intention, theological accuracy, it can be misconstrued. All truth is God's truth. Therefore, the 99 percent that is true is still from God. The falsehood or lie is only that one percent which is actually false. Of course, that one percent is usually about the nature of Jesus Christ, so it is of utmost importance.

Typically this phrase has been used to refute other religious beliefs and heretical teachings. However, it can misguide Christians into creating an all-or-nothing attitude in their conversations with people. For example, a person might think Buddhists are all wrong in everything because they are not Christian. However, Buddhists have some truth, because as Romans 1:18-25 states, the truth has been revealed to them as it has to us even in nature (we either believe that God's law is written on our hearts or not ... but we can't have it both ways). So a Buddhist can do what is moral and loving, just like a Christian. Unfortunately, the all-or-nothing attitude also creates an "us versus them" mentality—you are either with us or against us attitude—forgetting that God created all of us equally in His image.

What does Proverbs 18:1-2 say about the person who isolates themselves?

From what are they isolating themselves? (Hint: see v. 2.)

If you put together the teaching from Proverbs 12:15 and 18:1-2, what could you say about a person who doesn't listen to others' advice?

We must listen to others to keep ourselves accountable for what we believe and for what we think. If we become unwilling to listen and accept correction, Solomon says we show ourselves to be fools.

How easy or difficult is it for you to accept correction or criticism?

What are some steps you can take toward becoming better at receiving correction?

CONFIDENCE BUILDER: As part of our ministry of conversation, we are going to practice listening. The best way to learn is by throwing yourself into the fire. Ask a person with whom you disagree on an issue to explain their position as well as they can for the amount of time available. Do not interrupt them. When they are finished pick one thing they said and ask for better clarification on that point. Offer them a statement of "I can see how you could come to that conclusion. Thanks for sharing your view with me. I'm in Bible study where we are learning to listen to people better." Do not offer anything in return unless you are asked for it.

If you are not yet ready to go into the fire, practice listening to a radio program or watching a news show with views you oppose. Listen to try to understand their point of view. Do not let your opinion on the matter interrupt your listening. Thinking about how we disagree or how we'll respond is counterproductive to our current goal. To aid in listening, take notes.

When the person is finished speaking, say to yourself or aloud, "I can see how you could come to that conclusion. Thanks for sharing your view with me." Try to figure out a question on one of the main points for further clarification. You don't have to go out of your way to practice; the nightly news or talk shows will work just fine.

Remember the goal as you practice is to become a better listener so that you hear the person before answering them. Not many people in my experience do this activity very well (Christians included). When we don't listen well, we may come across as defensive, overbearing, insecure, or another undesirable trait. This is not a good, nor effective, testimony to the love and power of God.

What are some problems you foresee for our faith conversations if you are unwilling to have your beliefs corrected or criticized?

Obviously, we must strike a balance between accepting everyone's criticism and rejecting everyone's criticism if we are going to have great conversations. That is why you need to be skillful in handling the doctrines of the faith as well as in listening.

You need to be confident in your beliefs to confidently engage in discussion with others who will criticize them. Note that I used the word, "confident" and not the phrase "arrogantly dogmatic" or "exasperatingly belligerent." There is a difference. The first one is part of being a good ambassador for Jesus Christ. The latter ones can be conversation stoppers. The first one is still open to learn from others; the latter are closed off from further learning.

DO YOUR BEST TO PRESENT YOURSELF TO GOD AS ONE APPROVED, A WORKER WHO HAS NO NEED TO BE ASHAMED, RIGHTLY HANDLING THE WORD OF TRUTH. 2 TIMOTHY 2:15

As part of a lifelong journey of discovering truth, we should expect to find those people who have studied an area much further in depth than ourselves. If we aren't willing to listen to them, we'll miss opportunities to grow in our knowledge.

DAY THREE

LISTENING TO AVOID SPREADING UNTRUTHS

KEY POINT: We should attempt to really hear and understand a person's argument so we do not falsely testify about their position.

Today's concept is simple, yet it can be life changing. We are going to learn to listen with the express purpose of understanding the other person's view as the other person understands their view. You do not have to agree with them, but you should never try to make their argument fit what you want it to be. This seemingly simple task eludes many of us.

One of the most difficult conversation practices is to represent another person's view accurately. We often hear only what we want to hear, or we distort the other person's view so we can more easily tear it down. As Christians trying to share the truth, we cannot afford the practice of building straw men.

STRAW MAN = changing or exaggerating a person's position or argument to make it easier to refute.

CONFIDENCE BUILDER: Though I try to encourage Christians to attend public, formal debates on issues concerning belief in God, some have told me they do not like public debates. One reason given was that the debaters tend to misrepresent each other's views and then declare a hollow victory over each other's arguments. So nothing is really accomplished except tearing down each other's character. Basically, the complaint is that the debaters are not really listening to each other (a common complaint concerning relationship and marital arguments, too). While it is true that some debates can end up this way, it is not the rule. The current slate of debaters—Christian, Muslim, and atheist—offer an array of profitable and courteous exchanges. The Veritas Forum at Harvard University was created for the purpose of these effective interactions on this issue of God. You can find numerous free debates and lectures at *http://www.veritas.org.* I recommend beginning with Gregory Koukl, Michael Licona, Norman Geisler, or Ravi Zacharias.

Let's look an example of a straw man statement from Hans and Nathaniel Bluedorn's book, *The Fallacy Detective.*

> FATHER TO DAUGHTER: **Your mother and I have decided that we don't want you to date when you are this young. When you are old enough, we believe there should be some parental supervision.**
>
> DAUGHTER TO FATHER: *Oh, now I understand. You're going to make me sit up in my room all my life until you pick out somebody for me to marry.*[2]

What were the two parts to the father's original statement?

What did the daughter say in response?

How did the daughter change or exaggerate her father's position?

What was wrong with the exaggeration?

Write out the definition of a straw man.

When addressing a person's argument, we must listen carefully to what they are saying and make sure we attempt to understand their point of view. Otherwise, we could be misrepresenting their view as badly as we saw the daughter misrepresent her father's position. What's wrong with misrepresenting a person's view? It is making a false statement or even giving false testimony; it's an untruth. Untruths never lead us toward God. Read 1 Corinthians 13:6.

> [Love] does not rejoice at _____, but rejoices with the _____.

Why should Christians delight in the truth?

Christians claim that God is truth. His nature is truth and from Him all truth flows. Therefore His followers should love and earnestly seek what is true about everything. However, in my experience, we in the church have a particularly rampant habit of building straw men. We'll look at a couple examples.

> SUSIE-LOU-WHO TO CHURCH MEMBER: **I have been working with the pastor through some of the doctrines of this church of which I do not agree. He and I decided that since I couldn't reconcile my beliefs with this church that**

I should go where I could do so. He prayed for me about my decision and I left on good terms.

REPORTED BY CHURCH MEMBER: *Susie-Lou-Who wasn't in church today. She didn't agree with the pastor's sermon last week so the pastor told her to go find a new church.*

How did the church member exaggerate or change Susie-Lou-Who's position?

What should the church member have said instead to avoid building a straw man?

These two representations might seem close, but one of them slants the statement toward making Susie and/or the pastor look disagreeable and rash. This slanting makes it easier to write her off or blame the pastor, instead of responsibly interacting with the situation. Building a straw man thus replaces reporting what is true. In my experience, twisting of the truth like this goes on quite frequently in church, yet normally gets overlooked.

Why do we need to avoid building straw men between Christians?

What steps can you take to avoid building straw men in your conversations?

When we speak untruths about others we present a bad witness to those outside the church as well as those inside. Plus, it demonstrates that we're not really listening to others or trying to understand them. Now let's look at how further truth-twisting harms our ability to have faith conversations. Here is another example.

CHRISTIAN APOLOGIST TO CLASS: **Atheists are all fools, because the Bible says only a fool doesn't believe in God.**

This example is more difficult because we have no previous assertion to compare. Plus, this statement sounds similar to Psalm 14:1, "The fool says in his heart 'There is no God.' "

Can you think of why this might be a straw man? Be prepared to discuss your answers with the group.

GREG KOUKL of Stand to Reason Ministries, has written an excellent work on how to discuss your Christian beliefs with others entitled, *Tactics: A Game Plan for Discussing Your Christian Convictions.* This winsome and gracious way of talking with others will help you avoid creating and attacking straw men.

The "atheists are fools" example is a problem because the statement makes all atheists sound as if they are unintelligent or have silly reasons for rejecting God. This is a straw man because it fails to acknowledge more reasonable atheist arguments, such as "How can God be good with so much evil in the world?" It also stereotypes all atheists (a hasty generalization).

Straw men can create a problem for your church members when they try to talk with people of different beliefs. Can you imagine sitting down with your atheist friend and attempting to really listen to them when in the back of your mind you are recycling poor arguments like "all atheists are fools"?

Your atheist friend may have been hurt by a church or may have a reasonable question that you may miss if you are not intentionally listening to understand her point of view.

Why do we need to avoid building straw men with people of different beliefs?

How can you avoid building straw men about non-Christians when discussing their beliefs in church?

Avoiding straw men also has an extra, unexpected benefit. Ironically, few things help us communicate our points like making it clear that we understand the other person's points. Seeking to understand has a powerful impact on being understood.

Think of a time when someone showed you that they understood your point. What did that do to your willingness to hear what they had to say?

We see in the wisdom of Solomon that we need to first hear the other person in a way that we can speak uprightly and truthfully concerning a matter.

What does Proverbs 18:13 say about a person who answers before they hear?

What does "answers before they hear" mean?

Have you ever answered a person before you really listened to what they were saying? If so, what was the result?

Listening to understand requires more than just giving a person their turn to talk. It means that we need to truly hear their argument. We should then think carefully about our response before answering. Proverbs 15:28 says, "The heart of the righteous ponders how to answer, but the mouth of the wicked pours out evil things."

Have you ever told a person you would have to think on an issue before you could give them an answer? If so, what resulted?

What are the benefits of thoughtfully considering your response before answering?

Proverbs 15:28 contrasts the righteous who ponder how to answer versus the mouth of the wicked that pours out evil.

Why do you think Solomon draws a contrast between a person who thinks before he answers and a wicked person?

Our goal in a faith conversation is to discover truth. We want to be good advocates for truth. To do so, we have to try to understand the person's view. The first step we can take is to avoid building a straw man about their view or position. The second step is to really hear them out before answering. The third step we looked at was to think carefully about answering before we speak.

Write down one thing you can do this week to help you understand another person's view without building straw men.

A FALSE WITNESS WILL PERISH, BUT THE WORD OF A MAN WHO HEARS WILL ENDURE. PROVERBS 21:28

DAY FOUR

LISTENING FOR POINTS OF COMMUNICATION

KEY POINT: Through listening to others we can find productive points for discussion.

On a flight from Los Angeles, I met a man who said he was a Buddhist. I hadn't met a Buddhist before so I asked him to describe his beliefs. In the course of our conversation, he stated that he didn't believe such things as right or wrong. The way things are is just the way things are. Later in the conversation he said he thought the U.S. military involvement in a specific foreign country was wrong.

I remembered he had earlier said he didn't believe in right or wrong. So I asked how a Buddhist can think something like the military involvement was wrong if Buddhists don't believe in right and wrong.

He stopped talking and looked as if he'd never been asked that before. He said something like, "I guess I'm still working out my selfish desires."

When I got into this conversation, I decided to listen as intently as possible to this man as he described his view, because I knew somewhere along the way, I'd find something we could discuss in further detail. I found an error in his reasoning: As a Buddhist, he didn't believe in right or wrong, but when discussing military involvement, he thought something was wrong.

How is listening to people to find points of communication different than arguing?

What are some benefits of listening to find something you can discuss with a person who holds different views from your own?

Describe a situation in which you and a person you didn't know connected because you both had a similar interest or experience.

Did you find yourself much more engaged in conversation when there was a point of communication you both could discuss? Why or why not?

In general, people like to talk about familiar subjects. If you can spend some time to hear the other person discuss their beliefs, you will have a much better understanding of them and you will identify engaging material for both of you.

Many Christians seem to think they have to come to the conversation with a certain method of evangelism. They think that without this method, they cannot engage in conversation. While methods provide you with some good material and guidelines, they should not replace learning to be a good conversationalist who genuinely knows their faith and is genuinely interested in other people.

CONFIDENCE BUILDER: Have you thought about asking yourself, *Why do I believe in God?* Part of being a good listener is being confident in your own beliefs. To gain this kind of confidence you're going to need to articulate what you actually believe to be true about God. This means asking yourself to bear the burden of proof for your own beliefs. If you have never attempted to support your own belief in God, you may find it difficult to have a two-way conversation with those who adamantly oppose your beliefs. This may be because you do not know what you believe or why you believe it. So it becomes difficult to talk about your beliefs. Two great books to start learning some reasons for belief in God are Timothy Keller's *The Reason for God* and Lee Strobel's *The Case for Christ.* It really shouldn't take an atheist or Muslim to ask us to support our belief in God. As lovers of truth, this should be a task we take on ourselves before anyone asks it of us.

BUSY BEING DEFENSIVE

Sometimes Christians miss out on hearing points of communication with others because they become defensive too quickly and then fail to comprehend what is being said. When we let our emotions rule our conversations, we can miss out on the chance to have productive dialogue.

In explaining why it can be difficult to reason with some people, Dallas Willard writes, "Their very mind has been taken over by one or more feelings and is made to defend and serve those feelings at all costs."[3] He further says of our emotions, "Feelings live on the front row of our lives like unruly children clamoring for attention."[4]

(Day 4 continues on p. 66.)

ERRORS IN REASONING / LOGICAL FALLACIES

Using good reasoning helps us to discover what is true about the universe and God. However, good reasoning requires that we exercise our minds—a part of loving God with our whole self. These are a few common and classic errors in reasoning. This list is not exhaustive. In fact, these are just the tip of the iceberg of mistaken forms of reasoning. For more resources, check out the end of this article.

Ad Hominem: when an arguer is guilty "of attacking his opponent rather than his opponent's evidence and arguments."[1] An ad hominem attack is a way for one person to discredit another person's attempt to argue for a position. It attacks the person's character and motivation, rather than attacking the actual argument itself. The expected outcome is that the hearers will no longer give an ear to the discredited person's position due to their ill will against her personally. Since this argument fails to address the actual issue(s) being discussed, it is an error in reasoning. For example:

• Dear Editor: I was shocked by your support of Senator Spendall's arguments for a tax hike for improving highways. Of course the Senator favors such a hike. What else would you expect from a tax and spend Purple-Party member?[2]

• Senator A has given us reasons for increasing the pay for military personnel. But we all know that Senator A has three sons in the military, so his family would benefit if their pay was increased.[3]

• I hear that the famous author, Chrysanthemum, is an evangelical Christian. I can't believe anything she says now.

Hasty Generalization: generalizing about a class based upon a small or poor sample. The hasty generalization fallacy normally involves two problems: too small of a sample and not a representative sample.

For example:
• This is the best study on apologetics ever!
• All atheists are fools. I just talked with an atheist, and he thinks the moon is made of cheese.

The first example was a hasty generalization, because I have not reviewed all of the studies written on apologetics in order to know if the study I just wrote is the best one ever. The sample size for my inference is too small. The second example is a hasty generalization because it is not a representative sample of atheists. One atheist is too small of a sample size to use as a reference for all atheists.

Genetic Fallacy: "condemning an argument because of where it began, how it began, or who began it."[4] This fallacy is the most common form of ad hominem today.[5] It fails again to actually deal with the argument itself. Instead, it is an attempt to undercut the argument solely based in the origin of the argument. It is called genetic because it address the genesis or origin of an argument. For example:

• You don't believe I should smoke because of your Baptist upbringing.

• Your Christian beliefs are wrong because you are from the South.

• You say that just because you are a man.[6]

• What do you know? You're only a teenager.[7]

Violating the Law of Non-Contradiction: something cannot be "A" and not be "A" at the same time. When a person makes an argument that fails to address this basic law of logic, they have made an error in reasoning. For example:

• All religions are equally true. Whatever you believe is what is right. (Some religions teach Jesus is God and some teach Jesus is not God. Jesus cannot both be God and not God at the same time.)

- Christian beliefs are true for you but not for me. (Christian beliefs cannot be true and not true at the same time.)

Straw Man Fallacy: changing or exaggerating an opponent's position or argument to make it easier to refute/refuting an unfairly weak or ridiculous version of your opponent's view. Straw man is an error in reasoning because it does not address the actual argument or position. It builds up another argument, a straw man, that may be close to the person's original argument but is not the argument itself. Then the person attacks the straw man because it is easier to defeat. For example:

- Chris: Why are you an atheist?
  Aaron: I don't believe in God because I cannot understand how a good God could allow so much evil and suffering in the world.
  Chris: So unless God makes everything wonderful for you, you'll never believe in God. How foolish!
- Mrs.: Our car isn't running right. I think we need to buy a better one—something more comfortable.
  Mr.: Oh, so you want us to buy a brand new fancy car? I don't think we have enough money for a Rolls Royce.[8]

Red Herring: the introduction of an irrelevant point into an argument. "Someone may think (or they may want *us* to think) it proves his side, but it really doesn't."[9] As the authors of *Asking the Right Questions* remind us, "You should normally have no difficulty spotting red herrings as long as you keep the real issue in mind as well as the kind of evidence needed to resolve it."[10] The listener should ask themselves: 1) *What was the questioned asked?* 2) *What kind of response would specifically answer the question?* 3) *Did the response given specifically answer the question?*

The main reason a red herring is fallacious is because changing the topic of discussion does not count as an argument against a claim. For example:

- Son: Why can't I go see *The Day of the Spatulas* with my friends?
  Dad: Isn't there some other movie you could go to see instead?[11] (Dad is not answering the son's question. He moved to a different question.)
- Son: Why can't I go see *The Day of the Spatulas* with my friends?
  Dad: Why don't you go ask your mother?[12]
- Christian: Why do you believe God does not exist?
  Friend: How can you believe in a God that condones a barbaric practice like slavery?

RESOURCES FOR FURTHER INVESTIGATION:

The Fallacy Detective
by Hans and Nathaniel Bluedorn

"The Nizkor Project" Web site on fallacies,
www.nizkor.org/features/fallacies/

Asking the Right Questions
by M. Neil Browne and Stuart M. Keeley

"Your Logical Fallacy Is" Web site with a free downloadable logical fallacy poster,
http://yourlogicalfallacyis.com/poster

How can our feelings be like unruly children clamoring for attention?

Do you tend to react defensively when someone challenges your beliefs? Why or why not?

What can you do if you find yourself responding with defensive feelings toward a challenge to your belief?

You do not have to let emotions win the day. Let that initial reaction of heart-pounding defensiveness wash over you and roll back out. Take a moment to remember to focus on the content of what was said. Ask a clarifying question such as, "Did I hear you correctly when you said … ?" Many times, people are making errors in reasoning when they discuss belief in God, but we must be listening for them.

What was the error in reasoning the man made in our conversation on the plane at the start of the lesson?

The man demonstrated that he could not live by his professed belief system. He didn't believe in the existence of right or wrong, but he said he thought something to be wrong. Even the choice of being Buddhist would assume that Buddhism is "right." His view was self-contradictory. I may have missed this point if I had been busy trying to think of what I was going to say or if I had quickly become defensive. Let's look at some other errors in reasoning for which we should be listening.

COMMON REASONING ERRORS

In your group this week plan to discuss this list of common reasoning errors and definitions. Try to think of examples of each to discuss.

Ad hominem

Hasty generalization

Genetic fallacy

Law of noncontradiction

Straw man

Red herring

In your group seek to share non-blaming examples of these reasoning errors. Remember, the point is not to win arguments but to genuinely help people find the truth.

DAY FIVE

....

LISTENING IN PRACTICE

....

KEY POINT: We must put into practice good listening skills to see change in our conversations.

We have spent this week learning to listen with certain goals in mind.

Write out each day's title here and state the specific goal of each day in your own words.
1) Listening to

2) Listening to

3) Listening to

4) Listening for

What is one thing about listening that you learned this week; something you may not have thought about before?

How will this one thing affect your interactions with people of different beliefs?

I wish we had an entire study on this one subject. Over and over I find that we don't want to spend the time to listen and truly hear others. This understated aspect of conversation can build up relationships or tear them down and even harm our witness for Christ.

In our last day this week, let's focus on making a real change in this one area of our lives. Don't make the task of becoming a good faith conversationalist too big so that it seems insurmountable. Just take one piece at a time. This week commit to making the change in your listening habits with just one person.

Who is the person you will commit to listen to more carefully this week?

Now that you're committed to a change, let's look at some basic reminders to help you put good listening into practice.

PRACTICAL METHODS

We are going to start with the list of "do's" and "don'ts" when it comes to listening.

DO

1) Look people in the eye, unless this is a culturally unacceptable practice. In westernized nations, the person may view the inability to look them in the eye as being unsure or uncomfortable in the conversation. I realize some people are painfully shy, but we still need be mindful of body language and the message it portrays about our beliefs. If you are shy, practice by looking at your eyes in a mirror, then move to a family member's eyes. Here again, you can use television shows to practice.

You don't need three minutes of unbroken connectivity but a long enough connection to listen to an idea. You can look away to formulate thoughts, but then look back to their eyes. Also look them in the eye when you are speaking about your beliefs.

2) Be still when others are talking, preferably with arms down at your sides in a stance of confidence. This posture can be disarming because nothing is "protecting" you from them, such as crossed arms. It demonstrates that you are confident in yourself and, in this case, in your beliefs.

3) Make a concerted effort to remember a person's main points. If you are not good at remembering:

- First, try to get better by making a concerted effort to remember.

- Second, keep a small note pad with you to write notes for important conversations.

- Third, repeat a person's statements back to them to check for accuracy.

DON'T

1) Bird-eye around the room. A bird surveys the surrounding area for predators, dangers, and food. That's normal for a bird but not for a person having a conversation about their faith. Keep your eyes calmly rooted on the other person's face and eyes.

2) Pace and fidget. Pacing and/or fidgeting can be just a habit, but they can also convey nervousness. Either way, these practices can send a signal of irritability and they do not convey confidence.

3) Interrupt a person. We've already covered this in day 1, but it's very important to demonstrate respect for that person. Of course, if you get into a conversation with a person who just wants to steamroll you and not let you talk, you may have to interrupt at some point. In that situation, the other person isn't being respectful.

Greg Koukl has some gracious ways of handling a steamroller. He suggests that you say, "I'm not quite finished" when interrupted. If she interrupts again, say, "Is it okay with you if I take a few moments to answer your question before you ask another? I'll give you a chance to respond when I get done. Will that work?" Another effective statement is "That's not a simple issue. I need a moment to explain myself. Is that okay?"[5]

4) Think of your response while another person is making an argument. You will miss out on what they are actually arguing if you are formulating a response instead of trying to understand their argument. This is not so easy as it may sound. Once you gain some understanding of a basic argument—say against God's existence—you might tune out an individual who is using this argument as soon as the person begins to use it. At this point, you are not hearing them anymore. I have been guilty of this very thing. I'll assume I know their argument before they finish stating it. This assumption has caused me to be ineffective in conversations at times. It has also caused me to answer a question completely wrong in front of a group of people.

Write out the do's and don'ts of listening we have reviewed.

Which is the most problematic don't for you?

Which one of the do's are you good at?

How can you handle a person who won't listen to you, a steamroller?

When we engage with people we should always treat them in a manner worthy of the Lord Jesus Christ, even if they are being irritable or aggressive. In the Scriptures, Peter explains that our actions and words should be given in a manner that even those who would abuse us will bring shame upon themselves.

WHO IS THERE TO HARM YOU IF YOU ARE ZEALOUS FOR WHAT IS GOOD? BUT EVEN IF YOU SHOULD SUFFER FOR RIGHTEOUSNESS' SAKE, YOU WILL BE BLESSED. HAVE NO FEAR OF THEM, NOR BE TROUBLED, BUT IN YOUR HEARTS HONOR CHRIST THE LORD AS HOLY, ALWAYS BEING PREPARED TO MAKE A DEFENSE TO ANYONE WHO ASKS YOU FOR A REASON FOR THE HOPE THAT IS IN YOU; YET DO IT WITH GENTLENESS AND RESPECT, HAVING A GOOD CONSCIENCE, SO THAT, WHEN YOU ARE SLANDERED, THOSE WHO REVILE YOUR GOOD BEHAVIOR IN CHRIST MAY BE PUT TO SHAME. FOR IT IS BETTER TO SUFFER FOR DOING GOOD, IF THAT SHOULD BE GOD'S WILL, THAN FOR DOING EVIL.
1 PETER 3:13-17

As we bring this week to a close let's connect the arguments for belief in God in week 2 with listening skills in week 3.

Pick one of the arguments from week 2 that you are going to keep fresh in your mind so that you can utilize it this week as you listen for a point of communication. I'll give you an example.

Argument: Christianity encourages a concept of tolerance that surpasses the current cultural view of tolerance.

Listen for: any comments made that suggest the only real tolerance is accepting all views as equally true or that Christianity is an intolerant religion.

Your argument of choice:

What you will listen for:

Pray that God would put someone in your path with whom you can have a great conversation.

QUESTIONING OTHERS

GROUP

What are some steps we can take to become better able to receive correction?

What examples have you seen of people building straw men? What is wrong with the straw-man approach?

How is listening to find points of communication different than listening to argue?

What can you do if you find yourself responding with defensiveness?

Talk about the "Errors in Reasoning" article on pages 64–65. What was helpful? With what do you struggle?

VIDEO GUIDE

How to convert atheists:

1. Be _____.

2. Don't be _____.

Don'ts:

1. Don't tell atheists _____ _____ _____.

2. Don't evade serious _____.

3. Don't assert things you _____ _____.

Do's:

1. Explore the _____ openly.

2. Admit _____.

3. Come _____.

4. Gently point out the _____ in the atheist's reasoning.

Christians are not asking enough _____.

If a person must give _____ for their thinking, they learn the art
of _____.

We learn what we believe when we have to _____ _____.

Favorite question: What do you _____ _____ _____?

Since I began studying apologetics, I have noticed that Christians are engaged in a lot of defending and supporting their own beliefs. This is a good and productive activity. However, I haven't noticed as many Christians engaging others and encouraging them to support and defend their beliefs.

We seem to have become caught in a way of seeing the world that suggests Christians (or religious followers, more broadly speaking) are the only ones responsible for evidencing their beliefs. This is entirely untrue. Everyone has beliefs. We can productively and effectively question those beliefs.

This week we will add to our good listening skills and to our foundation of belief in Jesus, the ability to be good questioners who do not assume that others have reasoned through their own beliefs. Our model for asking valuable questions comes from Jesus.

* ● * ● ●

DAY ONE

JESUS ASKED QUESTIONS

Jesus used questions to challenge His followers as well as to confront those who opposed Him. Sometimes His questions helped the hearer discover a deeper truth about faith in God. At other times His questions served to expose an untruth and/or the person's dishonesty. Let's see an example where Jesus asked a question. Read Matthew 22:41-46.

To whom was Jesus' first question addressed?

What did Jesus ask?

What was the reply?

A couple groups of religious leaders had asked Jesus a series of theological questions just prior to Jesus asking this question. The purpose of these questions was to entrap Jesus to answer in a way that either violated the religious law or violated logic.

Jesus, knowing their dishonest intent, asked them a series of questions that would not only reveal an untruth but would reveal that these religious leaders were knowingly committed to falsehood. So far, Jesus had asked them who the Messiah would be and the religious leaders answered, "the son of David" (v. 42), in other words, purely a man.

What question did Jesus ask next?

75

What was the response to Jesus' question?

Why do you think the religious leaders responded this way?

Jesus, quoting Psalm 110:1, asked the leaders how it was that David could call a man who was David's son, "Lord." Plus, this "Lord" is the Lord who sits at the right hand of God: it is God Himself. This presented a logical problem if the religious leaders considered Messiah as only a man.

Jesus' questions revealed several problems for these religious leaders. First, they did not understand their own Scriptures (see Matt. 22:29). Second, Jesus demonstrated that the religious leaders were committed to an untruth. They would not listen and take to heart Jesus' theologically and logically accurate teaching. They were unwilling to change. Nor, as we see in verse 46, were they willing to face the truth at all; they stopped their interaction with Jesus.

Jesus used questions to draw out deep, personal bias in the religious leaders against His teachings and against His identity. He showed them that their beliefs were not rooted in good arguments or good reasoning.

Have you come across a person who was not making a good argument against the Christian faith? What was their argument?

How did you respond to their argument?

Have you ever been asked a question about your faith that was meant to entrap you? If so, what was that question?

How did you respond?

Have you ever asked a person a question to help them discover a problem with their reasoning? What did you ask?

When people ask us questions based in poorly-reasoned arguments, we can learn from the example of Jesus. Not only should we be able to demonstrate problems in the argument, but we should be prepared to ask questions in return. This can be an especially good learning experience, not just for the people engaged in the conversation, but for those who are listening in. This secondhand impact has been a by-product of some of my conversations.

I meet a lot of people on planes because I am a frequent flyer. On one flight, I was seated between two businessmen who had like-minded religious beliefs and who adamantly opposed mine. They team-attacked my beliefs the entire flight, but I kept asking them questions as well as answering theirs.

During parts of the conversation, the gentlemen were fairly belligerent, somewhat condescending, and even rude. At the end of the flight, after the gentlemen had left, as I was grabbing my suitcase from the overhead bin, I felt a hand on my shoulder. I turned to see a young woman with tears streaming down her face. She simply said, "thank you" without showing any intent of conversing with me further. Though the apologist in me desired to know what part of our conversation had affected her, I never found out. I couldn't find her after I got off the plane.

What do you think could be some reasons for her reaction to our conversation?

Have you ever taken time to notice how others respond to your conversations? What have you noticed?

We need to remind ourselves that our conversations can have an impact on people we never expect to impact. Jesus was always cognizant of the crowds.

> **"THE EVIDENCE** is there for all to examine. We can examine it defensively and miss the truth. Or we can examine it honestly and humbly, and discover the truth, believe, and be saved. The religious leaders were so blinded by tradition, position, and selfish pride that they could not—and *would* not—see the truth and receive it."[1]

4

DAY TWO

CHRISTIANS SHOULD QUESTION BELIEFS

SOMETIMES THE KINDEST THING WE CAN DO FOR PEOPLE IS GENTLY SHAKE UP THEIR PRESUPPOSITIONS AND INVITE THEM TO THINK.[2]

In 2007, I spoke at the University of Houston, Clear Lake, on "Can Truth be Known About God?" Some of the main points included:

1) We have a responsibility to find what is true.

2) To say you have truth is not intolerant.

3) Truth to be known does exist.

After my talk, several students asked questions, including one gentleman who talked with me for nearly half an hour. He was a follower of Eckhart Tolle, the main religious instructor in Oprah Winfrey's life at that time. His main question was how I could claim to know truth at all through my thinking abilities. He said that I couldn't know the truth about God until I got beyond my thinking abilities to the point where I experienced God as feeling, not as believing.

I said, "Can I ask you a question?"

He affirmed that I could.

"How do you know you have the truth about God?"

He replied, "Because I can feel it."

I asked, "But how do you know that feeling represents the truth about God?"

He thought for a moment. He said, "Because it is a good feeling."

I asked, "How did you decide that good feelings are equivalent to the truth about God?"

He said, "I don't know, but it's not something you decide by thinking about it."

"How do you decide something if you aren't think-ing about it? Did you think about Eckhart Tolle's ideas before you accepted them as true?"

I wasn't trying to confuse the gentleman or to frustrate him, but I noticed a problem in his view of God and truth.

What do you see as a problem in his view?

How would you have responded to the theory that a person cannot know truth about God until they get beyond their thinking abilities? Plan to discuss this concept with your group.

By asking a few questions, I uncovered a major inconsistency in this man's view. He believed you couldn't know the truth about God if you were using your thinking ability, but he had to use his thinking

ability to decide that his belief was true. This is a self-defeating statement—a statement that "fails to meet its own standard."[3] The man's statement about "getting past" thinking refuted itself because it required him to think to make the statement.

How would you explain to a friend the idea of a self-defeating statement?

What did the man say that was self-defeating?

Why does his statement defeat itself?

Why is it important to point out inconsistency problems in a person's worldview?

HERE ARE SOME OTHER EXAMPLES OF SELF-DEFEATING STATEMENTS:

"TRUTH DOES NOT EXIST."
– This is supposedly a statement that is true.

"THERE ARE NO ABSOLUTES."
– This is supposedly a statement that is absolute.

"I DO NOT EXIST."
– You must exist to say this.

"SCIENCE IS THE ONLY WAY TO KNOW ANYTHING."
– The statement cannot be proved scientifically.

My goal in the conversation with the man was to point out that his worldview was unlivable, because it had vital inconsistencies at the core of its teaching. I wanted to share with him the truth about his beliefs so he might be open to investigating them. However, I did this by asking him questions so he could discover the problems through his own thinking. I don't suppose I moved him to belief in Jesus as his Savior that day, but I hopefully planted a seed of doubt about his current view of God.

Out of great love for people Jesus invited them to examine their beliefs and their way of thinking to uncover truth. An instructive example of Jesus' concern for truth is the story of the rich young man. Read Mark 10:17-27.

What did the young man ask Jesus?

How did Jesus reply?

Even though Jesus hasn't directly addressed the man's point of how to inherit eternal life yet, Jesus has already questioned one faulty view—that Jesus is simply a "good teacher." People today continue to make this common mistake about the person of Jesus—that He could have been a good teacher but

"GOOD TEACHER": The Jewish rabbis at the time of Jesus would not allow themselves to be called "good." This was due to their understanding of the nature of God: that only God is good. The young man's label of "good" here was most likely intended to flatter Jesus as a rabbi, again exposing that the young man had problematic thinking; that such flattery could earn him points in the Kingdom.

At times, this passage has been used to show that Jesus Himself did not believe He was God. For instance, Muslim debaters will use this passage against the deity of Christ. However, notice that Jesus never refused the title of good teacher. He only questions why this man calls Him a good teacher. Jesus is looking for the man's understanding of Jesus' nature. Plus, Jesus implicitly teaches that He is God by His statement that none is good except God while not refusing the title of good teacher. Remember, rabbis would not accept this title in

Jesus' day; it was reserved for God alone. So Jesus cannot be a good Jewish teacher by accepting this title unless He was the actual good teacher as God.[4]

Further, after Jesus told the man what he still lacked to inherit eternal life (an insight into the man's heart), Jesus added that the man must come and follow Him (v. 21). Part of the answer to salvation was to follow Jesus. When taken in context, this passage becomes clear as support for Jesus' deity.[5]

not God. Jesus replies to the man's flattery by saying no one is good except God. Jesus is indirectly teaching the man the nature of His identity as God, who is the source and standard of goodness.

After Jesus' response that the young man must keep all the commandments, how does the man reply?

What does Jesus tell him to do?

Why does Jesus tell him to do this?

The man had a faulty and superficial view of salvation. He thought a person could be good enough to merit salvation. Jesus handled this falsehood with His former claim that no one is good but God, but then He takes another step toward opening the man's eyes to truth. Jesus confronts the man with a penetrating look into the truth of his inward state: that his allegiance was to wealth and not to God.

How did the young man respond to the conversation?

You and I shouldn't expect that everyone with whom we uncover deep truths will respond to the salvation offered through Jesus Christ. Sometimes, as in the case of the young man, people will walk away from the truth; especially when they have strong commitments to their beliefs already. Saint Augustine wrote:

THEY HATE THE TRUTH FOR THE SAKE OF THE OBJECT WHICH THEY LOVE INSTEAD OF THE TRUTH. THEY LOVE TRUTH FOR THE LIGHT IT SHEDS, BUT HATE IT WHEN IT SHOWS THEM AS BEING WRONG.[6]

How should we respond when people walk away from our conversation unconvinced?

THEODORE ROOSEVELT has been quoted as saying "Nobody cares how much you know, until they know how much you care."[7] It's a euphemism for those people who prize knowledge or position over their care and concern for others. Our goal in studying apologetics is not simply to gain a head swirling with knowledge. The goal is to gain knowledge of our beliefs that transforms our very soul; to where we begin to see exactly those people who need our care that we've been missing all along. Caring for others should be a hallmark of the Christian life. Our search for truth must be coupled with a character of kindness. Otherwise, our words will sound as a "clanging cymbal" in a raging world.

From the first part of verse 21, we see that Jesus loved this young man. He was obviously a spiritually-minded, moral person who eagerly desired to know what was true about God and salvation. But this man couldn't face the cost of what he desired.

Notice that though Jesus loved the man, He did not change the way to God for him. He would not change the truth for him, but out of love for the man, Jesus helped him uncover what was true.

You and I will not be able to reach into the mind and heart of any given person as Jesus did here. However, we can demonstrate a great love for someone by gently and graciously exploring their ideas. We can point out untruths we find in their view of the world. If they walk away unconvinced, we must trust in the sovereignty of God and the power of the Holy Spirit to rightly deal with each member of His creation.

One of the more difficult issues for Christians is to figure out how far we go in a conversation before we concede with a person to "walk away." What are your thoughts?

As you may have noticed, Jesus didn't chase the man down. He didn't continue to hurl Scripture quotes at him as he was walking away. This doesn't mean we should give up on a person, but it does provide an example for us.

Jesus does not verbally beat people down with what is true (or send them a barrage of text messages or Internet communication). He provides an opportunity for them to encounter the truth. There will come a point in some conversations or relationships when you must be willing to let that person make their decision even if it opposes your belief. And you must still love them. (Remember Luke 6?)

What impact do you think we have on others when they know we disagree with them but we are willing to investigate truth with them and continue to love them?

Now that we've established some of the reasoning for why we should question others, we'll begin asking those questions in tomorrow's study.

Think of someone in your experience who represents your example of the rich young man—someone who has walked away and who you cannot control. Below write your prayer for him or her.

DAY THREE

....

QUESTIONS TO GET YOU STARTED

....

At the beginning of the study, I asked what you would do if you and your family were discussing church at dinner when suddenly one family member stated, "Faith is a lack of critical reasoning." If you don't remember what you said, look back at your response on page 12.

After the study we've done together so far, how would you respond today?

Typically, most people would feel the need to respond to such an assertion with an argument. Today, however, we're going to look at a different kind of approach, a questioning approach. Instead of thinking we must be prepared to respond to anything thrown our way, we need to learn to question what we hear people say.

By asking questions, we can better understand a person's belief and we can help the person better understand their own belief. We'll break our questions down into a few basic kinds: what, how, why?

WHAT?

One of the most helpful questions you can ask a person is "What do you mean by that?" You might actually assume a person means something that they do not mean. Asking her this question gives her a chance to clarify her statement. By getting a clarification, you can better respond to her specific argument or belief.

This question will help you stay on target better by narrowing the focus of the conversation. It also helps to tone down any negative rhetoric that might

be contained within the statement. If a person is being sarcastic or caustic in their statement, you can quickly turn the conversation in a lighter, more profitable direction by asking what they meant.

Write the first question we learned.

Name three ways this question is helpful to our conversations.

1)

2)

3)

To demonstrate how the questions can be effectively utilized in a conversation, we'll build an example conversation through all of our questions. Here's my example of the first question.

> **FRIEND: I am against religion because it teaches us to be satisfied with not understanding the world.**

> YOU: *What do you mean by that?*

> **FRIEND: I think religious people believe in spite of the evidence.**

At this point in the example conversation, we can see that the first statement was quite broad and could go several directions in philosophy, theology, or a specific field of science. However, with a clarifying question, we now have a narrower field of discussion. The friend's specific concern is what we might call "blind faith." At this point we could offer an answer of how faith and reason traditionally go hand-in-hand in Christianity. Or we could ask another question.

CONFIDENCE BUILDER: Faith and reason are not opposites. Faith and no faith are opposites. Reasonableness and unreasonableness are opposites. As we saw earlier in our study, not even Jesus Himself expected His followers to exercise blind faith with no reasons or evidence to believe He was God. We looked at the passage from Luke 7:18-22 in which even John the Baptist had doubts about Jesus as the Messiah. When John's disciples questioned Jesus, He apparently allowed them to see Him perform miracles of healing as physical evidence of His claim. Then Jesus sent them back to John to report the evidence they had seen.

Faith is also common among all humans. Faith is more like trust and confidence than it is like Mark Twain's "believing what you know ain't so."[8] All people exercise faith in themselves, in one another, in institutions and ideologies, in the practice of science, and in the business of life. Think about how impossible our day would be if we had to fully evidence everything we do or say to avoid utilizing any kind of faith. We might not be able to even get out of bed in the morning.

The Christian faith is better described as knowledge that leads to understanding that leads to belief that leads to trust and confidence in God. Philosopher William Lane Craig stated, "Christian faith is not an apathetic faith, a brain-dead faith, but a living, inquiring faith. As [Saint] Anselm put it, ours is a faith that seeks understanding."[9] It's difficult for people to believe something that they think is absurd or that lacks any evidence whatsoever.

HOW?

The next question we can utilize is "How do you know that?" Instead of immediately taking up arms against a person who has made an objection to the Christian faith, make them support their statement.

Sometimes you will find a person has actually studied what they believe but not as often as you might think. In my experience, most people I talk with face-to-face have not spent a considerable about of time grappling with their view of God. You might be assuming way too much about the other person's knowledge when speaking to her. She may not have taken the time to really investigate a belief. Rather, she may have adopted this statement because it fits with what she wants to be true. This question will help you find out how she has come to her current conclusion.

Write the second question we learned.

Name some benefits of asking this question.

Let's use the next question in the example conversation we are building.

> **FRIEND: I am against religion because it teaches us to be satisfied with not understanding the world.**

> **YOU:** *What do you mean by that?*

FRIEND: I think religious people believe in spite of the evidence.

YOU: *How do you know that?*

FRIEND: None of the Christians I knew were able to answer my questions. They would tell me that I needed to have more faith, they would change the subject, or they would say the question was inappropriate. One guy even told me that I just wasn't serious about God and that I was probably bound for Hell!

What do you see as the friend's actual issue?

If you hadn't asked the questions, would you have responded differently to the first and third statements by the friend? How?

What is one thing you can do to help this friend now that you know more about the problem?

What other question can you ask this friend?

Now we are beginning to see the actual problem more clearly. The friend had questions that her Christian friends couldn't or wouldn't answer. She learned to equate the faith of Christians with the lack of desire or inability to find answers. Since we now know the real issue, we can offer her help in a way that would be effective for her: we can offer her help in finding those answers. If she brings up numerous questions, ask for the most important one and tackle that one first.

Another option would be to pursue the logical problem she has created. She told us that people of religion believe in God in spite of the evidence. Her basis for that statement was her own experience with believers. She made a hasty generalization, painting all religious people as the same as the relatively few Christians she knew. After gently pointing out the flaw in her reasoning, we could ask something like this: "What Christians have you read or heard about who do answer really tough questions? Would you be willing to read through one of their books with me?"

Other forms of the basic "How" question:

1) How did you come to that understanding (about God, religion, social issue, etc.)?
2) How do you know that is the truth?
3) How have you come to this conclusion?

Write the two basic questions we learned today.

1)

2)

Why is it important for us to ask questions first rather than to jump into responses?

Now we have two basic questions we can use in our faith conversations with others. These questions can begin to change not just the conversations we have but how we view those conversations as well.

One woman who had attended a couple conferences of mine in Texas told me that these questions had completely changed the dynamic in her office. She said the environment had gone from one of hostility toward Christians to one of excitement to discover and discuss beliefs. That's exactly what we are shooting for.

I AM FINDING more stories of people who left the Christian faith because they had difficult questions no one would answer. But I'm also seeing stories in which the person left the faith because they noted an attitude of apathy toward critical thinking among the body of Christ. Kenneth Daniels, the child of evangelical missionaries wrote a book about his reasons for leaving his faith, *Why I Believed: Reflections of a Former Missionary.* He states, "In all my years of faithful church attendance, Bible studies, Christian college, missions training, and seminary, I do not recall one sermon, not one injunction encouraging me to examine my faith critically."[10]

DAY FOUR

QUESTIONS TO GET YOU STARTED, PART 2

Yesterday, we learned a couple of questions we should ask when engaged in a faith conversation.

Say both questions out loud to yourself or to someone else.
• **What do you mean by that?**

• **How do you know that?**

Try to find a moment in your conversations today or tomorrow to ask at least one of these questions; whether it is of a family member, friend, Christian, or someone else.

Our next question should become a staple in our arsenal of questions. In week 2, we asked the question, "Why do you believe that?" of ourselves and we took time to review the basis for our own beliefs. This week we are going to take the same question and begin asking it of others.

WHY?

When we ask a why question, we are not just asking the person for the "how did you get here" trail of evidences; instead, we are further inquiring of how those evidences led to their trust and confidence in that view. We want to get at the motivation for their personal decision to hold to this view.

This inquiry can provide a lot of common ground material to discuss: background situations such as family issues, church problems, doubts, professors who challenged their faith, and much more. It will hopefully get us to the ultimate reasons for committing to a particular position.

Write the third question we learned.

In your own words, what is the difference between asking "How do you know that?" and "Why do you believe that?"

What is one benefit of asking this question?

You may also find that a person doesn't know why they believe something to be true. To be honest, this happens to all of us many times. We don't spend all our time figuring out why we believe every little thing we believe. However, when it comes to figuring out the big things, such as the worldview that structures our whole life, this is an endeavor vital to our successful living. Many Christian apologists and philosophers alike have shared Greek philosopher, Socrates' sentiment, "The unexamined life is not worth living."[11]

What is the value of knowing why we hold to our beliefs?

What could you say to a person who is apathetic about their reasons for belief or disbelief? Be ready to discuss this in your group.

CONFIDENCE BUILDER: Every person has a view of the universe: ideas about the origins of the universe, human ancestry, life after death, and the existence of God. Christians are not the only people with a view. When talking with others, we must remember that they have a view about God and about the universe that needs to be supported with evidence and reason. It is not solely the task of Christians to evidence and reason a view of God and of the universe. Now, get out there and ask about what people believe and why they believe it!

Let's look at a possible example of this question in a sample conversation.

> **FRIEND: I am against religion because it teaches us to be satisfied with not understanding the world.**
>
> YOU: *What do you mean by that?*
>
> **FRIEND: I think people of religion just have faith; they believe in spite of the evidence.**
>
> YOU: *How did you come to that conclusion?*
>
> **FRIEND: None of the Christians I knew were able to answer my questions. They would tell me that I needed to have more faith, they would change the subject, or they would say the question was inappropriate. One guy even told**

me that I just wasn't serious about God and that I was probably bound for Hell!

YOU: *So you are saying that if Christians are willing to answer your questions then you wouldn't have a reason to say they believe in God in spite of the evidence.*

What is the friend's claim for why people believe in God? (You may have more than one answer.)

FRIEND: **No, I would still say they believe in spite of the evidence**

YOU: *Why do you believe that?*

FRIEND: **Because we do not need to say there is a God in order to explain things. We are too intellectually sophisticated for that sort of superstition anymore.**

What was different in the answer to the why question from the previous questions?

In the "how" response, the friend claimed that Christians believe in spite of the evidence. She thought Christians didn't really look at evidence as a basis for belief in God.

She changed directions with response to the "why" question. This question revealed that she thinks Christians need to say they believe in God—

FALSE DICHOTOMY (DILEMMA): "When someone asserts that we must choose between two things, when in fact we have more than two alternatives, he is using the *either-or fallacy.*"[12] The false dichotomy is also called the "either-or fallacy " because it usually states that we choose either this or that.

In the sample conversation, the false dichotomy was set up when the friend implied that a person is either an intellectual or believes in God. Though it was not stated quite so explicitly, this is an error in reasoning because another option exists: you can be an intellectual who believes in God.

Another false dichotomy in her statement was that you are either superstitious if you believe in God or not superstitious if you don't believe in God. However, people who don't believe in God can be superstitious and people who believe in God may not be superstitious.

perhaps as an emotional need—to "explain things." She likened this need to superstition and contrasted the need to the sophisticated intellect. It seems this friend has set up a false dichotomy assuming that intellectuals have no need of God and/or that believers are not intellectual but merely have felt needs that are further based in superstition.

What would be a good follow-up to her response?

By asking these questions we have come to a position of much more clarity. First, we narrowed the statement on religion to a discussion on Christianity. Second, we have some background on how it was she came to reject the Christian faith. Third, we have found out why she ultimately rejects Christianity. Now we have much material to discuss with our friend and we did all of this by asking her questions rather than jumping into the conversation before we had a better understanding.

She perceives that Christianity is all about meeting some kind of emotional or perceived need, possibly based in superstition. If Christianity is all emotions-driven, then there is no reason to think that it promotes exploration of the universe and advancement of our understanding of anything that is not emotionally driven.

Now we can focus our response to her specific misunderstanding: that Christianity is all emotion-based. A good quick response to her would be, "I do not need to say there is a God, I think good reasons exist to believe in God. Would you like me to explain what I mean by that?"

A further explanation could include the necessity of God's existence, how He has revealed Himself to mankind, and what He did to solve the human condi-tion (the problem of evil/sin). We could ask a couple of other questions at this point in place of repeating "What do you mean by that?" We can soften the questions we ask.

SOFTENING OUR QUESTIONS

In his book, *Tactics*, Greg Koukl offers a couple of questions to use that may come across as less direct.
"Have you ever considered that … ?" and
"Can you help me understand this?"[13]
Both alternatives help to soften the force of the question and keep the conversation more amiable in nature. You could ask variations of these two questions specific for our sample conversation.
"Can you help me understand what kind of things God explains according to your statement?"
"Have you ever considered that many highly intelligent, nonsuperstitious people believe in God? What do you think about their belief?"
"Can you help me understand how faith is opposed to reason?"

Using ideas you've heard from your own interaction with people, write some of your own examples of these last two questions.

We need to be prepared to ask people questions when we hear their statements about belief in God. The longer we wait to respond, the more awkward and contrived it will sound. Our goal is to have natural conversation with others. So, to be ready, we are going to have to practice using the questions.

DAY FIVE

PRACTICING OUR QUESTIONS

Let's quickly review the three basic questions from this week's study.

Write out three basic questions to use in conversations.

1)

2)

3)

Think of some other forms of these questions and write them here.

What are two questions you can use to soften the questioning approach?

1)

2)

In the next section, you'll see some statements that I have encountered either in person, online, or through reading. We'll use these statements to practice asking our questions from this week's study.

After each statement, write a question you could ask for further clarification. You may use any of our basic questions or you can write them using your own wording (personalized).

THE UNIVERSE WE OBSERVE HAS PRECISELY THE PROPERTIES WE SHOULD EXPECT IF THERE IS, AT BOTTOM, NO DESIGN, NO PURPOSE, NO EVIL AND NO GOOD, NOTHING BUT BLIND, PITILESS INDIFFERENCE.[14]

THE BIBLE MAY, INDEED DOES, CONTAIN A WARRANT FOR TRAFFICKING IN HUMANS, FOR ETHNIC CLEANSING, FOR SLAVERY, FOR BRIDE-PRICE, AND FOR INDISCRIMINATE MASSACRE, BUT WE ARE NOT BOUND BY ANY OF IT BECAUSE IT WAS PUT TOGETHER BY CRUDE, UNCULTURED HUMAN MAMMALS.[15]

NERDY TECH TIP
I like to use whatever is at my disposal to help me practice good conversation. One great device available to help us practice is the smartphone. If you have no one who can ask you the questions you can record these with your phone. Play back the voice recording pausing in between each to ask a question.

RELIGION IS THE ROOT OF ALL EVIL.

RELIGION HAS RUN OUT OF JUSTIFICATIONS. THANKS TO THE TELESCOPE AND THE MICROSCOPE, IT NO LONGER OFFERS AN EXPLANATION OF ANYTHING IMPORTANT.[16]

Now that you've written out some responses, it is time to begin verbalizing your questions. You will need to get a partner to help you with the next section. If you don't have anyone who can help you, then you're going to have to do some role-playing. One person will read the lines below and you will respond with a question (don't peek ahead … try to do them as you hear them).

[THEOLOGY] IS IGNORANCE WITH WINGS.[17]

WE DON'T NEED GOD TO BE GOOD.

WE ARE ALL ATHEISTS WHEN IT COMES TO MOST OF THE GODS. I JUST GO ONE GOD FURTHER.[18]

JESUS DOESN'T SAY IN THE BIBLE, "I AM GOD, WORSHIP ME."[19]

IT'S UNJUST FOR SOMEONE TO DIE FOR THE SINS OF ANOTHER.

GOD ISN'T SOMETHING YOU BELIEVE IN; GOD IS SOMETHING YOU FEEL.

SCIENCE IS THE ONLY MEANS WHICH HUMANS HAVE TO KNOW TRUTH.

ALL THINKING MEN ARE ATHEISTS.[20]

Let's take our questions to the next level. Write down some objections you've heard to belief in God or objections to Christianity (or perhaps your own doubts or questions).

In your group session, be prepared to use these objections to practice some questioning dialog. Get two or three people together and use the objections you've heard to help another woman in your group practice her questions. If you want to try to play devil's advocate and reply to each other's questions, invoking a follow-up question, that would be great. However, be sure to be considerate of each person's confidence level at this point. Not everyone will be up to playing devil's advocate just yet.

STAYING ON TARGET

You may have noticed that our sample conversation took a few major turns. It began with the idea of religion being opposed to learning (generally speaking), then it moved to the subject of faith versus evidence, and eventually got to the subject of science.

You may also encounter responses as meandering as our example. As a general rule, though, try to use questions to focus on the premises in the first statement you hear. This helps the conversation stay productive by circumventing potential rabbit trails. Let's see what this would look like in our example conversation.

> **FRIEND: I am against religion because it teaches us to be satisfied with not understanding the world.**
>
> **YOU**: *What do you mean by that?*
>
> **FRIEND: I think people of religion just have faith; they believe in spite of the evidence.**
>
> **YOU**: *I'm sorry I meant to ask you what do you mean that religion teaches us to be satisfied with not understanding the world?*
>
> **FRIEND: Religion is based in faith, which doesn't requiring understanding.**
>
> **YOU**: *How do you know that? How do you know faith doesn't require understanding?*

This is now a very narrowly focused conversation that will get at the basis for the friend's original statement. Her next move is probably to argue that faith

is opposed to reason or something similar, but she's going to have to base her argument in some kind of evidence: evidence that faith doesn't require reason.

Where is she going to get that kind of evidence? Is she going to quote a scientific study? Probably not. Will she be offering a philosophical argument concerning faith and reason? Again, probably not. Most likely this is the point at which:

1) her argument will break down and hopefully she realizes her argument lacks evidence, or
2) she begins to put "all power to the shields" to deflect incoming truth missiles (a little Star Trek lingo for any fans out there), or

3) you may have to agree to disagree. If she responds with #1, then you might be able to go into the argument for why the Christian faith is based in reason and evidence that lead to understanding. If #2, then you may consider using a softening question such as, "Can you help me understand why it is that faith in God doesn't require understanding?" This may also be a place to cease the pursuit of her argument in hopes of having another conversation. If #3, you are stepping away to give each person a breather, and that's OK. Usually this step results from an unexpected escalation in emotions but can also be the result of discerning a hardened heart and closed mind.

What is an advantage of keeping our questions aligned with the originally stated idea?

What is one way you can further a conversation when a person begins to get defensive?

How do you know when it is time to step away from a conversation?

CONFIDENCE BUILDER: Most people have not spent time deep in philosophical and theological arguments to be able to academically engage on the topic of faith and reason. You will not get an argument based in an actual philosopher or theologian's work 99 percent of the time. Usually, you will get sound-bite theology or sound-bite philosophy based in pop culture; for instance, a sound-bite of popular atheist author Richard Dawkins. Do not assume anyone knows anything. Always ask questions.

If you do come across a well-informed person, who can argue the philosophy or theology involved, consider it a great opportunity to learn from them. Ask them specifics about the concerns of the particular philosophers or theologians of whom they quote. Ask them why they believe this person is correct. Ask what is the best refutation of that view on the matter. Tell them you appreciate their time in helping you with an area of which you are not as learned. Ask for sources for recommended reading on both sides of the issue. If the person is someone you will see again, ask them if you can have some time to digest the material and then come back with more questions. If you will not see them again, you can ask to exchange e-mails so you can look into the material and get back with them; or you can say, "I appreciate your help in this area. I plan on looking into the material."

REFLECT

As you begin to ask questions of people and engage in conversation, you will probably notice that you are not an expert at conversing right away. Don't be discouraged. Use each conversation as a chance to learn and grow. After a conversation, you may want to go back over the discussion in your mind and think of better questions you could've asked.

Think of one person in particular of whom you wished you had an answer the last time you got into a conversation on beliefs. Think back over the conversation. What question would you ask them now?

Pray now that God will place people in your path of whom you can begin to ask questions about their beliefs. Commit to practicing your questions so you are ready for conversation anytime and anywhere.

HOW BEAUTIFUL UPON THE MOUNTAINS ARE THE FEET OF HIM WHO BRINGS GOOD NEWS, WHO PUBLISHES PEACE, WHO BRINGS GOOD NEWS OF HAPPINESS, WHO PUBLISHES SALVATION, WHO SAYS TO ZION, "YOUR GOD REIGNS." ISAIAH 52:7

RESPONDING TO OTHERS

GROUP

How would you respond to the theory that a person cannot know truth about God until they get beyond their thinking abilities?

How would you explain to a friend the idea of a self-defeating statement?

What are your thoughts about how far we go in a conversation before we walk away?

What are some benefits of asking, "What do you mean by that?"

What are some benefits of asking, "How do you know that?"

What is the difference between asking "How do you know that?" and "Why do you believe that?"

VIDEO GUIDE

Action 1: Show the person the _____ with their statement.

- _____ errors in reasoning.

- _____ recognition of errors.

- _____ the other person.

Action 2: Respond to valid _____ concerning Christianity.

- Realize that _____ _____ exist in many fields.

- Saying, "I don't know" demonstrates _____.

- Churches should be a _____ _____ for hard questions.

In an emergency, the first people called are termed first responders. They are available quickly and always ready. They carry basic emergency equipment because they never know when they will be called, but they do expect to be called.

As Christians, we should train ourselves, in a way, to be like the first responders. We should be available quickly and always ready to give an answer (remember 1 Pet. 3:15). We never know when we will be called, but we should have some basic equipment available assuming we will be called.

In this week's study we'll develop our "basic equipment": how to respond to others. This is the fourth part of our faith conversation.

• • • •

DAY ONE

BE READY

In week 1, we saw Peter's admonition to a group of persecuted Christians that they always be ready to offer a defense of what they believed about Jesus Christ (see 1 Pet. 3:15). If they trusted Jesus as Lord, these persecuted Christians should set aside their fear of man, specifically when it came to giving reasons for their belief in God. They were told to always be ready.

Apologists, studying the defense of our beliefs, have often cited this passage. However, other passages invite us to engage in reasoning what we believe; for ourselves and for others. For example, read Isaiah 1:18.

To whom God is speaking (see vv. 1-17)?

What does He invite them to do?

This passage is specifically inviting sinful people to come to their senses and admit wrong in their attitudes and practices. God calls them out to reason or argue with Him concerning their wrong thoughts and actions. This call was specific and general. It was both specific for the nation of Judah, but the general principle is for all sinful mankind.

Why do you think God called sinners to reason with Him regarding their sin?

According to verse 17, what is the goal of reasoning with God?

We want others to find the salvation in Christ that washes "scarlet" sins as "white as snow." Because God calls man to reason, we too, can engage in reasoning with others for the purpose of helping them discover the truth that leads toward salvation.

In this Isaiah passage, God argued the truth of the sinful nature. We also have the challenge of arguing for the sin nature in our current times. According to Christian apologist C.S. Lewis, "To bring this doctrine into real life in the minds of modern men, and even of modern Christians, is very hard. ... Christianity now has to preach the diagnosis—in itself very bad news—before it can win a hearing for the cure."[1]

This should not be a discouragement to us but an encouragement that we have much to discuss in our day. Sometimes we will be discussing hard questions, such as the problem of evil. Other times, we will be discussing basic problems, such as errors in reasoning. Both are equally important. Let's look at why you need to point out errors in reasoning.

GENTLY POINT OUT ERRORS

Proverbs 14:12 tells us "There is a way that seems right to a man, but its end is the way to death." We have a responsibility to warn those on that way.

I participate in a lot of discussion about beliefs via the Internet. One day, an atheist gentleman sent me a comment that was not well reasoned, nor very courteous. His comment was, "Since you are an apologist, you will be twisting the truth. Every apologist twists the truth and is dishonest. I've never even HEARD of an honest apologist, so I don't expect you are ... so rather than debate, I thought I'd just let you know the utter disdain I have for you and your kind. Otherwise from your little cocooned world you might think everyone agrees with your nonsense."

Do you see any problems with his reasoning? What problems did you find?

HANS AND NATHANIEL Bluedorn, *The Fallacy Detective*

M. NEIL BROWNE and Stuart M. Keeley, *Asking the Right Questions*

"THE NIZKOR PROJECT" A Web site on fallacies, *www.nizkor.org/features/fallacies/*

"YOUR LOGICAL FALLACY Is" A Web site with a free downloadable logical fallacy poster, *http://yourlogicalfallacyis.com/poster*

I responded first by welcoming him to the group discussion on which he posted. Then I began to point out several errors in his reasoning. (Check back to week 3, day 4 for specific errors in reasoning). He had committed ad hominem by saying I was dishonest. He used the genetic fallacy by stating that truth will be twisted if it comes from an apologist. He used a hasty generalization by saying that every apologist twists the truth and is dishonest.

Once I had pointed out some issues with his reasoning I encouraged him to engage in questioning any of the arguments I had made on my Web site. I suggested, "I will still offer a response to an actual argument." Instead of taking up the offer, he responded with more negatively charged fallacies and with a shocking admission. He said he wasn't claiming to have used logic at all!

Why do you think this gentleman claimed not to be using logic?

What would you say in response to his claim?

What would you say to a person who said something like, "I'm being illogical"?

To ask such a question may seem odd. Yet, as you study how to make good arguments, you will more often recognize when people make bad arguments or refuse to engage in good reasoning. Another part of being ready to respond is preparing to face unreasonable people.

My response to his statement was, "This isn't good. I think you want to show people on my page that I'm wrong. To do so, you will have to make reasonable arguments and use evidence." As we've seen, Jesus pointed out errors in reasoning when speaking with those who opposed Him.

I eventually had to reply to this man that I wouldn't continue to engage in conversation with him unless he stopped the ad hominem attacks and fallacious statements. Teaching people how to be polite and reasonable conversationalists—good ambassadors for their own worldview—was an unexpected part of the defense of my faith. I had to say, "You may be a pretty great guy, but you haven't allowed me the chance to get to know you."

GENETIC FALLACY: condemning an argument because of where it began, how it began, or who began it.

The gentlemen who said to me, "Since you are an apologist, you will be twisting the truth," committed a genetic fallacy. He was condemning my arguments because the arguments were coming from me, an apologist. He was not condemning my arguments due to any problems with the arguments themselves; such as poor reasoning. This is an error in reasoning, a logical fallacy.

> **LOGIC:** is the system of thinking properly, of arriving at proper conclusions. There are formal laws to logic, but for our purposes we can understand it at this more basic level; logic is good thinking or good reasoning. For an argument to be sound it must use logic. But, if you're having a hard time wrapping your head around what logic is, then think about what it isn't. We call something that doesn't make sense illogical, or not logical.

What do you expect to be a challenge for you in responding to people?

What can you do now to be ready to respond to a person who isn't making a good argument?

Write out one way to point out an error in reasoning without coming across as disrespectful or angry.

DAY TWO

BE AVAILABLE

After I doubted my belief in God and then returned to believing in Him, I began to say a prayer every week for one specific thing. I don't remember the exact wording, but it was similar to: "God use me; I want to be used for Your work in my lifetime." I had concluded that since God was real, I wanted to be a part of anything He was doing.

Until now, I haven't told many people about this prayer. It had never been something I thought was important to share. Plus, being the skeptic that I am, I don't want to force a "connect the dots" between what I am doing now and that prayer back then. However, I am confident of one thing, and I'll risk sounding cliché to say it: I wasn't particularly able to do apologetics at that time, but I was available and willing. I wanted to learn and I desired desperately to be a part of whatever God was doing in this world.

People such as Christian philosophers and seminary professors have training to respond to difficult questions about Christianity. However, they may not be as available to people we know, like our friends, family and co-workers. This is where you and I can make a difference as available first responders. When Jesus called His "first responders," He called people of different backgrounds with different abilities, but all were available. Read Matthew 4:18-22.

Who does Jesus invite to follow Him (four people)?

What was their response?

How long did it take them to respond?

The story of Jesus calling the first disciples does not tell us much about their background or what their concerns might have been: whether they were concerned about their reputation or their jobs. This story focuses on their response. They responded immediately. Let's look at one more disciple's calling. Read Luke 5:27-28.

Who did Jesus ask to follow Him and what was this man's profession?

From what you know, what is significant about society's view of Matthew's profession?

Tax collectors were not well-respected people. They were known as crooks, for exacting extra taxes, and for pocketing the money for themselves. So Jesus is not going after the elite, eloquent, nor even the people we'd typically think of as good people. These fishermen and the tax collector were average, unremarkable, and in need of forgiveness. But they were also ready, willing, and available. Therefore, Jesus could use them to change the world (see Acts 17:6).

Do you ever consider yourself "not good enough" to talk with people about God? Why or why not?

Have you ever worried that if people knew who you really were they'd think you're a hypocrite? Have you not been talking with people about God because you fear your life isn't a good witness? While these issues may or may not plague you, I can say with certainty these issues plague many Christians. I've talked to believers who struggle with such feelings and dealt with these thoughts myself.

Some of us have heard the saying by Ghandi, "I like your Christ. I do not like your Christians. Your Christians are so unlike your Christ."[2] Others have heard similar statements that keep them from even beginning to give answers to people. This is wrong thinking. None of us will ever be good enough to perfectly represent God; remember God offers us salvation through Christ because of our imperfection and sin. We aren't and can't be good enough in what we do when compared to the perfect God.

Instead of waiting for the perfect time to respond to people, or until we feel ready, we need to begin immediately. Experience is the best teacher and certainly makes the most lasting impression. If you do poorly in responding to someone, learn from your experience and be open to changing your method next time around. As G.K. Chesterton noted, "If a thing is worth doing, it is worth doing badly."[3]

What can you do to get past an instance when you didn't do well in a conversation?

This happens to me, too! I go back over in my mind what I could have said and/or done better to respond or interact with the other person. Sometimes, I will write down better responses. Overall, I try to use each situation as a learning experience, even if my end of the conversation wasn't very well done.

Name some of the people you have contact with everyday.

Do you think they perceive you as being available to discuss belief in God?

If so, how have you made yourself available to others? What specific things have you done? If not, how can you make yourself a person who is available to others?

CONFIDENCE BUILDER "I lost my faith in January 2008. Now, I'm an outspoken advocate of rational thinking and naturalism."—Common Sense Atheism[4]

In atheist Internet ministry, the author and/or webmaster often has a similar statement to this: "I used to have faith. I now advocate rational thinking." This is a logical fallacy and Christians need to call it out wherever they see and hear it. It is a false dichotomy.

The idea of rational thought is difficult to explain outside of belief in God (or gods, for the pagans). Christians and Jews believe that God has made them in His image, with certain qualities that reflect the greater qualities found in God. This creation includes God's ability to think rationally. So we believe in the ability to think rationally about the universe because we believe this ability was created by a rational being (God) who is beyond the subjectivity of the human mind. Thus we have a reason to ground rationality as a "real thing."

Atheism has no such God. Rationality in an atheistic worldview must come solely from humanity. It could be a product of biological evolution. It could be a delusion. We could just be the lucky animals that eventually were able to reason. However, since rational thought is necessarily bound to the human animal it is not something that can be proved to be a "real thing." It is a product, or by-product, of our evolution, which may be a result of natural selection. This hypothesis does nothing to ensure that rational thought is not some sort of delusional trickery or that the world we are thinking of is real. We have no means to check how we know that rationality is informing us accurately about the world. This is a problem for atheism not found in the Jewish, Christian, or Muslim worldview. Do not be quick to allow the atheist to assume that rationality is a weapon in their arsenal. They must provide a logical argument, with evidence, to support this claim.

"Reason is itself a matter of faith. It is an act of faith to assert that our thoughts have any relation to reality at all."[5]

Before I studied my reasons for belief in God, I wasn't all that ready and available. I had reservations about talking about beliefs. Part of that reservation came from allowing too much influence from my culture (the idea that Christians are naive and ignorant party poopers) and not enough thoughtful interaction with deep thinking about Christianity (Christians have a solid foundation for a flourishing human life). This created in my mind an imbalanced view of Christianity and belief in God.

We must continually strive for balance in our daily lives, including the balance of our responsibilities to work and family with our responsibility to attend to our thoughts and beliefs.

We are eventually going to be faced with difficult questions about this life, either from ourselves or from others. Are you ready to respond? Let's continue this week to work on putting some more equipment in our basic first responder's bag.

DAY THREE

....

BE HONEST

....

Back in my public school teaching days, I had the responsibility of disciplining my band students when they broke the rules. Usually, this entailed a discussion between a student and myself in the band office. One particular "Mrs. Sharp lecture" I gave to students was on integrity. I used to tell them, "It's very difficult to earn a person's trust back after you've destroyed your integrity with them."

When we engage people in faith conversations, it is vital that we maintain our integrity. Once we lose trust, it is very difficult to earn it back. You can lose a person's trust in different ways.

Name some ways you can lose a person's trust in a conversation.

We can lose it by saying one thing and doing another—hypocrisy. However, all people are hypocrites at some point in their life because no one is able to "keep the whole law" (Gal 5:3). So we lose integrity when we fail to recognize our own state of hypocrisy at times.

We can lose a person's trust by not demonstrating an honest interest in them as an individual. God loves people right where they are in life; no matter where that may be. When we treat a person like a conversion project, this could send a message that they are only valuable to us if they either become a Christian or are on the path to becoming a Christian.

Name two ways to demonstrate honesty to others.

In your own words, describe how to handle the problem of hypocrisy in your own life.

How might we lose a person's trust if we treat them as a project?

Another way we can lose a person's trust is failing to admit when we do not have the answers to their questions. In John 14:6, we learned that Jesus called Himself the way to Heaven. However, He also called Himself "the truth." When we talk to people about Jesus, our subject matter is "the truth." We must be truthful in our conversation. Since none have God's knowledge—all knowledge of every possible subject—we cannot expect to have answers to everything we might be asked. This is an honest position to take about our beliefs.

Why is it impossible to have the answers to every question that we are asked?

In writing to Titus, who is teaching in Crete (read Titus 2:1-8), Paul reminds Titus what it means to teach sound doctrine and all that goes with it. Paul says Titus should demonstrate integrity, dignity, and sound speech for the purpose of offering no opportunity for his enemies to speak evil of him.

What does Paul tell Titus to show in his teaching in verses 7-8?

What reason does Paul give for these aspects of teaching?

DO WE TREAT people as projects? One complaint I've heard a few times from non-Christians is they felt like Christians only cared about them as long as they were having a discussion about belief in Jesus Christ. They felt they were someone's pet project instead of someone's beloved friend.

I've even been told in evangelistic training that the point to all of our conversations with nonbelievers is literally to share a presentation of the gospel story every time. The reasoning was that we couldn't guarantee another day of life for any given person. I might miss an opportunity to share the gospel with a person who could die tomorrow and then spend eternity in Hell. For me, this was a polarizing statement.

The pressure made me shut down my openness to discussion before I got started. I was worried about my presentation of the gospel. I felt inadequately studied to discuss biblical truths. I didn't want to lead someone away from the truth, so I left the discussion up to those whom I was convinced were more able than myself.

While there is a general truth behind the statement, it seems to put an inordinate amount of emphasis on conversion in comparison to the emphasis on love and compassion for God's creation. One agnostic friend shared with me that one reason Christianity was so attractive was because Christians accepted him for who he was, not for what he believed. He knew his

Christian friends would be there no matter what he decided about God. Christians give a powerful testimony when they trust God's sovereignty while effectively discussing the truth about God.

Not every situation will be the same, but remember to keep your intentions with individuals in check. The primary force behind sharing the gospel is love for others. It is not just to share what is true, because you think sharing truth, in of itself, is loving. For example, I could share that my friend's nose is crooked from a motorcycle accident. While it may be true, it may not be loving. Sharing the truth in love is a harmonious blend of compassion and verity.

CONFIDENCE BUILDER: The idea of the triumph of human reason over the mysteries of the universe developed from the Enlightenment era. It has led to some unreasonable expectations in our current era.

• First, that a person could possibly have 100 percent certainty with regard to any belief or any piece of knowledge. Even those things we have direct experience of, such as the breakfast we ate this morning, cannot be 100 percent proved.

• Second, that science is the only means by which humans can know anything. Famous physicist, Stephen Hawking, even mentioned this idea in his book, *The Grand Design.* No method of science can prove that the methods of science are telling us what is real.

Enlightenment philosophers, such as David Hume, assumed that everything we know is discerned through our five senses. Do you think he discerned this knowledge through one of his five senses? Of course not. His belief is self-contradictory, yet it still widely affects thought in our day.

When we do not speak with integrity, what happens to our relationships with others?

When we do not speak with integrity, what happens to our witness to others?

Think of three different ways a person can speak without integrity.

1)

2)

3)

Paul also included "sound speech" in his instructions to Titus. How is sound speech related to good conversation?

Why do you think Paul included "dignity" in his instructions?

Dignity means a "seriousness of manner, appearance, or language."[6] Not only did Paul want Titus to show he was trustworthy in his teaching but also that he was serious about his teaching. Sound speech shows that we know what we are talking about. As followers of Christ, one way we can demonstrate integrity, dignity, and sound speech is to be honest about our knowledge or lack of it. We don't have all the answers and we do make mistakes. If you are in a conversation with someone and you make a mistake, you must admit it for the purpose of maintaining the integrity and dignity of yourself, your message, and the person's perception of God.

Notice I'm not saying you have to be perfect in all your ways or in every situation. You just have to be willing to admit when you are wrong or when you do not know something. This small act of humility can prove to be very impacting on others.

Why is admitting when you have made a mistake important?

Is it difficult for you to admit your errors? If so, what steps can you take toward change?

Have you avoided conversation about God with non-Christians because you feel that you must have all the answers? Why is this a wrong belief?

At a women's conference in Oklahoma, I taught a session entitled, "The Redefining of Faith and How Christians Can Respond." At the end of my presentation, I opened up the floor for a question and answer session. One woman asked me a question I didn't know how to answer. I said, "I don't know, but if you're willing to e-mail me, I can find out." I didn't think much of my response until I found out later that another lady at the conference said that she had never heard a Christian say that they didn't know the answer to a question. It profoundly impacted her to hear a Christian say that they didn't have all the answers; that was one of her main blocks to belief in Jesus Christ. Who would've guessed that such a simple statement could be so powerful?

WHOEVER SPEAKS THE TRUTH GIVES HONEST EVIDENCE, BUT A FALSE WITNESS UTTERS DECEIT.
PROVERBS 12:17

DAY FOUR

BE DISCERNING

In responding to others, we've looked at being ready, available, and honest. Today we'll discuss a question people ask me nearly every time I speak on productive conversations: "How do I tell when the conversation is over or when I need to leave it?" Let's first look at a passage of Scripture often used to support a decision in this matter. Read Matthew 7:1-6.

How would you summarize Jesus' teaching in verses 1-5?

Typically, this passage is used to teach about judging others. What is a frequently heard teaching from this passage?

However, what is Jesus teaching about interacting with others, in general?

At the end of a passage typically associated with teaching the hypocrisy of judging others when a person has similar or worse problems themselves, we find a metaphor about dogs and pigs. I've heard this passage used to explain why some believers do not talk with atheists (especially angrier atheists). I've been told this is "casting pearls before swine." However, Jesus is not offering a justification for avoiding people here. Instead, He is teaching on appropriate responses based in well-discerned needs.

Jesus uses familiar imagery to teach His listeners to "discriminate between the holy and unholy to give what was appropriate where it was needed"—to the persons who would benefit from the gift.[7]

Set in context, the metaphor reads: We should not offer the holy meat intended for the priests to the dogs who more appropriately receive table scraps. We should not trick pigs—who expect edible food—by giving them inedible pearls, angering the hungry pigs. In both metaphorical situations, the example is an inappropriate response to the needs of the dogs and the pigs. Jesus was not calling the very people He had come to save dogs and pigs.

Part of learning to be a wise judge, one who is helpful to others, is to accurately discern needs and appropriately respond. This passage teaches how to be "wise and effective" in ministering the gospel.[8] We cannot use this passage as a means to rule out conversing with others, even difficult people. However, the passage does warn us that we must not use inappropriate means to help people.

For instance, if a person vehemently believes that the Bible is not sacred or not an authority, it would be inappropriate to dole out Scriptural reproofs on their lives and expect it to be effective like it would on a Christian. Instead, it would seem more appropriate to work with them on what they are trusting and whether or not that is a dependable authority.

CONVERSATION STOPPERS. Sometimes, people are going to be conversation stoppers. They are not interested in your point of view at all. If you attempt to pursue them, they may hurl insults at you and/or verbally abuse you and your beliefs. While it is disappointing that this happens at all, it does happen. We must move along and allow God to work on them. Otherwise, we really are inappropriately reacting to a situation—like the metaphor of dogs and pigs.

Also, this could be a chance to build a case for why the Bible is trustworthy as an authoritative work.

Viewed in this light, what do Jesus' words in Matthew 7:16 teach us to do in each circumstance we face?

If a person doesn't believe the Bible is authoritative or sacred, why is it ineffective to use Scriptural reproofs on their life?

What can we discuss instead?

Part of being discerning is learning to give appropriate answers to individual situations. Another part of discernment is learning how to gauge when to leave a conversation. Generally speaking, a person should reciprocate the parts of conversation we've learned up to this point. If a person is not reciprocating, it's probably time to wrap it up.

WHAT TO LOOK FOR IN CONVERSATIONS
As you begin to interact, others should be willing to:
1) Answer your questions.
2) Listen to your responses.
3) Interact with your responses.

ANSWER YOUR QUESTIONS
A person should be willing to listen to your questions and then actually try to give you answers. If a person changes the subject to a different objection or answers your question with a question, politely remind them that you have asked a question they have not answered.

This, of course, does not apply if they just didn't understand your question or need a clarifying point. For example if you asked, "What do you mean by that?" and they ask you, "What specifically are you looking for?" you shouldn't immediately assume they are not interested in an honest exchange of ideas. However, if the person continues to avoid answering you, they may not be interested in an open dialog. As there could be many reasons for their disinterest, it won't help to speculate. Specifically look for the avoidance of questions in assessing whether or not to continue in a conversation.

LISTEN TO YOUR RESPONSES

We dedicated an entire week of this study to learning to listen well. Admittedly, we are not all that great at listening all the time. So we can rightly expect that other people aren't the best listeners at times either. However, a person who is not the best listener is different than a person who doesn't want to listen or isn't even trying to listen.

While you are speaking, you should expect the other person to:

1) Look at you; not looking around at everything but you.
2) Remember your main points.
3) Attempt to properly represent your ideas.
4) Not think of their response while you are making a point.
5) Not interrupt you.

These are basic courtesies as well as signs of interest in a conversation. I'm particularly attentive to #3 when speaking with a person. If the other person in the conversation does not try to understand my argument as I understand my argument, then they might be looking to attack rather than converse.

We will experience misunderstandings at times due to the fact that we don't see things the same way. My concern is that the other person is trying to understand my argument from my perspective, not that they do understand it.

In week 4, we discussed how to handle a person who constantly interrupts you. Write down one way to handle an interrupter.

A lack of these signs may suggest that a person is not interested in what you have to say; another indicator that it may be time to finish the conversation and move on.

INTERACT WITH YOUR RESPONSES

In a healthy faith conversation, you and the other person will each offer ideas about why you believe what you believe. You should notice that the other person is engaging some of your ideas and commenting on them or even asking you questions about those beliefs. If the conversation becomes very one-sided, discussing only the other person's ideas—such as the conversation is all about objections to belief in God, but none of the reasons for belief in God, this is an indication that you need to wrap up.

Remember, a conversation involves two people. It entails at least two person's beliefs, not just one person's beliefs. You have value as a person, and your ideas and views matter too.

What is an indicator that a person is not interested in an open dialog on belief?

When you enter into conversation on belief, why should you expect the other person to interact with your views?

Through my ministry, my husband and I hosted a youth apologetics training camp. At the very end of the camp one year, I did a mock dialog with the students in which I role-played an atheist. I began by making some statements on why I do not believe in God and then I asked for questions. As soon as the questions began, I led the conversation off course.

Every time a student either asked me a question or offered me a response, I basically ignored them and moved to a different objection to God's existence. None of the students held me to a single argument or line of thought. As a result, our dialog was fruitless.

After nearly 10 minutes of meandering arguments, I broke character and asked the students why they were not holding me accountable to interact with their responses and questions. They didn't even realize they were doing so. There were about 20 of them altogether, and not one of them caught me.

THE SAWED-OFF SHOTGUN APPROACH

Lack of focus can be detrimental to a conversation. The dialog may include many things, but it usually gets nowhere on any one subject. I call this a "sawed-off shotgun" approach. It seems like the goal is to shoot at everything in a haphazard manner to hopefully hit something.

A sawed-off shotgun has a wider pattern than the regular shotgun, so the spray of damage is broader. This approach signals to me that a person doesn't want to be held accountable for any one argument or consider another person's ideas at any kind of depth.

When you encounter someone who sprays arguments all over the place without going into depth

on any one of them, try to get them to discuss only one argument at a time. Keep going back to that one subject; over and over. To do this isn't rude, rather it is an attempt to be effective in our communication.

Also, note that this approach is not specific to any group of people. Christians can also be guilty of utilizing the shotgun approach. If you have to handle a sawed-off shotgun person, try setting the parameters in advance of your discussion, such that the other person is prepared to discuss only certain subjects. You can remind them during the conversation if you get offtrack.

Have you ever been caught in a conversation in which a person seemed to take a sawed-off shotgun approach, arguing all over the place? What was the result of that interaction?

Why is it important in faith conversations to stay on a narrow course of discussion?

Think of some ways you can get back on topic if a person is not interacting with your part of the discussion. Write them here.

In Matthew 10:16, Jesus taught His disciples about the persecution to come as He sent them out to share the good news. In His teaching He warned that they should be "wise as serpents and innocent as doves." Though we do not have the same situation as the disciples—certainly not the persecution they experienced—we should still utilize Jesus' admonition in our daily interactions with others.

Don't just have discussions, but instead be wise and innocent with your discussions. Make sure your conversations center around the appropriate need of the person; lest we cast our pearls before swine. Also, avoid conversations that are going nowhere with a person who isn't really interested. Politely excuse yourself from a conversation if you notice it isn't productive or is inciting agitation.

Here are a couple of examples of what to say.

I appreciate your willingness to talk with me. I hope we can do this again sometime. Thank you.

I appreciate you talking with me. I am not convinced that your view is correct, but I want to give you the last word as we wrap it up.

The second example entails giving a person who isn't interested in your view the last word. This idea came from Koukl's book, *Tactics.* It's a gracious way to bow out of a conversation with a not-so-gracious person.[9]

Today we've considered situations where argumentation will not be helpful. Determining you should not continue a conversation does not mean you do not care about their salvation.

Brainstorm ways you can continue to humbly serve those who are unready or unwilling to have an honest conversation. Discuss this topic with your group this week.

LET US PURSUE WHAT MAKES FOR PEACE AND FOR MUTUAL UPBUILDING.
ROMANS 14:19

DAY FIVE

BE PREPARED

I've been asked a few times, "What do I say if I know I only have a short time to respond?" This question always poses a challenge for me, because you normally cannot satisfactorily respond to a statement with a quick quip. Yet, sometimes that is all you can do. So today we will consider a few quick responses to some popular sayings.

CAUTION:

Never use these quick responses without both understanding what you are saying and a true concern for the person. These are not mantras to zing a person and make you look good. These responses are to help you formulate a shortened version of a bigger argument. See page 111 for a list of resources available for understanding the broader argument.

Below you will see a statement in quotes followed by possible quick responses and a short explanation.

1) **"There's no such thing as truth."**
   - Do you think that statement is true?
   - If so, then even your statement isn't true.

The person making the statement that there is no truth must think that at least his or her own statement is true. Therefore, they do believe in truth, even if it is just this one truth. This self-refuting statement should be pointed out, as it is an error in reasoning.

2) **"That's true for you, but not for me."**
   - Is your statement only true for you, or is it supposed to be true for me as well?
   - If my belief is only for me, why isn't your belief only for you? Aren't you saying you want me to believe the same thing you do?
   - You say no belief is true for everyone, but you want everyone to believe what you do.

When engaged in a faith conversation, if a person tells you that whatever a person believes is true, they have committed an error in reasoning. The person making the claim believes that the claim is true for everyone, not just for those who want to believe it is true. Since the statement asserts at least one truth that is true for everyone—that there is no universal truth for everyone—this is a self-refuting statement.

3) "Christians are arrogant for trying to convert others to their view."
   - But isn't that your view of Christians and aren't you trying to convert others to this view of yours?
   - Are you arrogant, then, for trying to convert others to your view of Christians?

In attempting to dismiss Christians as arrogant for sharing their view of the world, the person has shared her own view of the world—specifically, her view of Christians. Therefore, the same standard (arrogance) would apply to her because she is attempting to convert others to her view. As Paul Copan states in *True for You, But Not for Me,* "Those who try to discourage or prevent others from evangelizing are themselves 'evangelists' for their viewpoint." He calls them "crypto-evangelizing" because it is evangelism in disguise.[10]

4) "People are atheists when it comes to most of the gods. I just go one further."
   - The Christian God lacks nearly any resemblance to the mythological gods, so I'm guessing you didn't just go one god further in disbelief.
   - I'd like to know specifically how you came to this conclusion. It seems highly uninformed about any of the gods.

This statement was made somewhat famous by the popular atheist author, Richard Dawkins. It relies on the argument that the Christian God is just another pagan mythological god; like Zeus or Osiris. However, the Christian God is so overtly different from these gods, that it is unlikely the person making the statement has really spent time researching the matter.

5) "Science is the only way we can know things."
   - Since no method of science can prove that statement, how do you know this?
   - How can you prove that statement is true through any method of science?

Anyone who believes the only things we know come through the methods of science has failed to understand both truth and science. Many of the unstated premises of science are not provable through the scientific method. All of the following are philosophical assumptions:
   i. the existence of truth
   ii. the laws of logic
   iii. that we can know the external world
   iv. the reliability of our cognitive and sensory faculties to gather truth and to justify beliefs
   v. the adequacy of language to describe the world
   vi. the existence of numbers and mathematical truths[11]

6) "To be good, we don't need God."
   - What do you mean by "good"?
   - People can aptly do good without believing in God, but people cannot aptly define good without believing in God. But no one is good.

Without God, we do not have a way to define the term *good*. Without God as the perfect standard of good, the term becomes subjective to whatever humans decide at any given time. So there becomes no such thing as a definition of good. No authority of good remains by which to make a comparison.

Good becomes a changing, shifting idea and relates to a social agreement as to what is good and what is not good. This paves the way for utilitarianism: what is good for the greatest number of people is good.[12] Under utilitarianism, many truly evil actions can be and have been justified as the greatest common good—for instance, the euthanization of the elderly, handicapped, or sick due to cost.

7) "All religions teach the same thing."
- Since even the most familiar of all the world's religions teach contradictory views of God in their basic doctrine, this is an uninformed statement.

In week 2 we looked over the idea that all religions teach the same thing. We know this is obviously untrue due to just the teachings on Jesus alone.

8) "Religion causes division and wars. It has been responsible for horrendous evil."
- One of the bloodiest centuries of all history was the 20th century. Much of the destruction was at the hands of atheist regimes; such those of Stalin, Mao Tse-Tung, and Hitler.
- Atheistic views also cause division and wars. Rulers holding atheist worldviews have led to some of the worst offenses against humanity: regimes of Stalin, Mao Tse-Tung, and Hitler, for example.

Atheism, when adopted as a philosophy for governing people, has led to some of the worst atrocities in mankind's history. A quick look into the statistics of atheist communist and socialist regimes of the 20th century will help with this sort of 21st century historical-philosophical-political amnesia. This is where agnostic George Santayana's statement, "The one who does not remember history is bound to live through it again" would be a useful reminder.[13]

PRACTICE

Now you need to practice speaking the responses. Words always sound different to me when they are said out loud versus when I am just thinking about them. It takes some practice to use an inflection of voice that will not sound accusatory nor defensive.

Practice these responses with a friend before jumping into the frying pan.

Remember the tip from earlier: if you have no one to help, record the comments on a smart phone or with your computer and play them back, responding to each one. The important thing is to say them aloud.

Think of a way to say the same ideas in your own words.

You never want to come across as giving a pat response or a prefabricated set of answers. You don't want to be fake. That is why the caution at the front end of today's study says that you need to understand the response before using it. If you have no idea what the response means, take some time to look at the further resources listed. A little study will yield great results.

Resources for further understanding:
- #1, #2, #3. Paul Copan, *True for You But Not for Me: Deflating the Slogans that Leave Christians Speechless* (see "Part I: Absolutely Relative")
- #4. Ronald Nash, *The Gospel and the Greeks: Did the New Testament Borrow from Pagan Thought?*
- #5. J.P. Moreland and Dallas Willard, *Love Your God With All Your Mind* (see chapter 7, "Apologetic Reasoning and the Christian Mind")
- #6. Greg Koukl, *Tactics: A Game Plan for Discussing Your Christian Conviction*s (see chapter 9, "Sibling Rivalry and Infanticide")
- #7. Doug Powell, *Holman QuickSource Guide to Christian Apologetics* (see chapter 5, "Which God Exists?"); Kenneth Samples, *A World of Difference*
- #8. Alister McGrath, *The Twilight of Atheism: The Rise and Fall of Disbelief in the Modern World*

· WEEK SIX ·

ROADBLOCKS

GROUP

How can we point out errors in reasoning without coming across as disrespectful or angry?

What are some ways we can lose a person's trust in a conversation?

What are the dangers of treating others as if they were projects?

How can we demonstrate integrity in conversations?

How can you get back on topic if a person is not interacting with your part of a discussion?

What are some ways you can continue to humbly serve those who are unready or unwilling to have an honest conversation?

VIDEO GUIDE

Roadblock 1: We live in a time that doesn't think truth about _____ can be _____.

"Almost every student entering the university believes, or says he believes, that truth is _____."[1]

We can know _____.

Roadblock 2: _____ hurt

Anything can become a _____ about God.

Get out there and get _____.

1. Allan Bloom, *The Closing of the American Mind* (New York: Simon & Schuster, 1987), 25.

Have you ever been driving and come upon a road-block? A roadblock is something that blocks progress or prevents accomplishment of an objective. You probably had to change your route to get to your destination. Normally, we don't give up on a destination when we hit a roadblock. Instead we figure a way to get past it. In our last week together, we are going to work through some roadblocks that we might encounter to discussing our beliefs so that we can get our faith conversations started.

* * * * *

DAY ONE

ROADBLOCK #1: YOU

From my own experience, and from listening to other women, I've found that we are one of our biggest problems for good conversation. We can be our own roadblock.

What are some of your hang-ups with talking to people? Which ones apply to you?

○ I'm an introvert.

○ I'm shy.

○ It's not my calling or my spiritual gift.

○ I don't want to impose on others.

○ It makes me feel weird.

○ I don't think they will listen to me.

○ My friends and family are not receptive (they're a unique breed of unreceptive gospel-rejecters).

○ I don't like confrontation.

○ I don't have time.

○ It's an imposition to me.

○ My focus now is: my kids/my job/my school.

○ I'm not interested in talking with others.

○ I'm too emotional.

○ Other people are not at my level.

○ I'm not smart enough.

○ I don't feel worthy to talk about God.

Why do you think these things keep you from conversing with others?

While these are legitimate concerns, they can keep us from ever talking with other people about God. A few of the previous concerns might even seem a bit hard to admit. For instance, who wants to confess that they are not interested in talking with others or that they think other people aren't at their level of knowledge? But these are thoughts that women do entertain. If we aren't honest about this roadblock, we aren't helping ourselves to get past it.

What can you do to get yourself past some of these hang-ups?

To get to a point of comfort in conversing, we are going to have to make an effort of some kind. We will have to do something. The roadblock of myself is one of the toughest ones. I struggle with it every day. Sometimes I just don't feel like talking with other people. Sometimes I struggle with apathy.

If you truly desire to be able to talk about beliefs, you must address this roadblock. You don't have to become a street-preacher every time you leave the house, but you have to develop receptivity to conversation with others.

In 2 Timothy 1:7-14 what kind of spirit does Paul tell Timothy that God has given us?

If we believe Paul's words then we need to get past the hang-ups that keep us hostage and prevent our acknowledging this power in our lives. The first step is to cultivate the desire to clear this roadblock. The next step is making small changes to get past it. The third step is consistent practice to work past it. The fourth step is looking back on who we were before and after this roadblock, reminding ourselves that we can easily slip back into old behaviors and attitudes.

List the four steps toward moving past this roadblock.

1)

2)

3)

4)

I used to be concerned that by telling people about Jesus, I was somehow imposing on them. I thought *Who am I to tell others what to believe about God?* Whereas, I was comfortable participating in group evangelistic events, my level of discomfort skyrocketed in everyday situations.

ON BEING SHY. One way to get a shy person involved in conversation is to have them enter the conversation after someone else has initiated it. If you are the shy person and another Christian is present, you can ask them to be the initial question-asker while you add to the conversation here or there. Maybe you can just be a responder at first.

I dealt with this problem inadvertently by studying apologetics thus solving my own doubt issues. Once I had confidence in my beliefs, that assurance bled over into confidence in conversing with others. This confidence-building is why our study in week 2 and our "confidence builders" are so important to having great faith conversations.

Write out something you hadn't been able to answer in the past but that you can now answer about your faith.

How does this help you in a conversation about God?

Pray that God will guide you to situations in which you can effectively use your knowledge.

DAY TWO

ROADBLOCK #2: OBJECTIONS

Yesterday we considered our fears and insecurities as the first roadblock to our faith conversations. The next roadblock comes from outside ourselves. The objections we will encounter from others represent our second roadblock. We've handled two kinds of objections throughout this study: the intellectual objection and the emotional objection.

> INTELLECTUAL OBJECTION: Rational justifications a person offers for why they do not believe in God. These objections can be based on inferences drawn from empirical data, for example the objection that Darwinian evolution makes belief in God superfluous and unnecessary. Or they can come from inductive or deductive arguments against God's existence, for example the problem of evil.

What is an intellectual objection to the existence of God? Write your own definition.

When someone has an intellectual objection, they may just need some answers to questions about belief in God. This may mean correcting false information or remedying misperceptions. It may also entail sharing new information of which the person had no previous knowledge.

Sometimes people hold an intellectual objection without even knowing why. So we might have to help

"THE FREEDOM FROM RELIGION FOUNDATION" (FFRF) uses the term "freethought" in many of its articles. However, in a search for a definition of freethought on their site, I found no definition, other than "free-thinkers: atheists, agnostics and skeptics of any pedigree." What I did find is a statement of purpose: "The purposes of the Freedom From Religion Foundation, Inc., as stated in its bylaws, are to promote the constitutional principle of separation of state and church, and to educate the public on matters relating to nontheism."[1] So it appears that this foundation is either confused or mixing in matters they claim they are specifically attempting to avoid: engaging the state in matters of the church.

The organization seems to have generally located their definition of freethought in relation to a position within the debate on the separation of church and state. This leads them to a non sequitur. I believe this is not their intention and they would

adamantly disagree with my assessment.

1) Freethought does not equal the separation of church and state. It should actually be defined as *thinking for oneself.* It has nothing to do with the debate on the church and the state. Neither does the term equal "nontheism." The term *freethought* contains an assumption that a person has free will—a theory borrowed from Judeo-Christian philosophy of the nature of man. The FFRF actually depends on biblical concepts as a source for free will. Without free will you cannot have truly free thought. Christians derive free will, and therefore freethought, from the nature of the Creator. Yet this group seeks to destroy freethought in the name of saving it. As G.K. Chesterton wrote, "It is absurd to say that you are especially advancing freedom when you only use free thought to destroy free will."[2]

2) By touting the terms "separation of church and state" the FFRF has missed

the broader underlying philosophical issue, which is about the state imposing a particular worldview on the citizen. By definition, atheism is a worldview; as is every other religion. The state cannot enforce the practice of atheism or even enforce the practice of the appearance of an atheist state according to the establishment and free exercise clauses of the U.S. constitution.

3) All worldviews have ethical implications when their theories are put into governing practices; as the writers of the Constitution clearly understood. In legislating laws, these worldviews must be treated equally as distinct ethical systems of belief—although worldviews are not equally ethically beneficial. In other words, none of these views get a free pass as innocuous systems of belief, since they all have moral implications. The FFRF fails to demonstrate even this basic philosophical understanding of worldviews and government.

the person figure out the source of their objection. The questions we learned in week 4 can help us find the source. When someone has an intellectual objection without a concurrent emotional objection, we can usually respond with good arguments and reason. By clearing away these arguments against God, you can help a person see that God is worth their trust.

Answers to intellectual objections to God might include:

1)

2)

3)

When a person doesn't know the source of their objection, what do you think we can do to help?

I noticed a new young man coming to church with his mother for a couple weeks in a row. When I asked about him, the youth minister told me I should meet him because he had some good questions. In speaking with the young man, I found out his major question was why he should choose Jesus when so many different beliefs exist in the world.

What would you have told him? Before looking ahead, write out your response.

I first acknowledged that he had asked a really good question. I suggested to him that I would base my religious decision on which belief system best fit with reality. He agreed.

We discussed the reality of the problem of evil and suffering in this world. We agreed that a belief system should adequately address and handle the problem of evil. Then I asked him if he knew how the major worldviews address the problem of evil (Hinduism, Buddhism, atheism, Judaism, Christianity, etc.). He did not.

So I asked if we could go through them briefly together. When we had finished our short survey of the different views, he told me that Jesus made a lot of sense. Later on, a youth worker visited him at his home and he trusted in Jesus as his Savior.

This man had an intellectual objection he needed to clear up so he would be ready to trust Jesus. However, not just the doubts of others but our own doubts can be a roadblock to conversation.

Do you still have intellectual doubts? What are those doubts?

What steps can you continue to take after this study to remedy your intellectual doubt?

Intellectual doubts will not go away on their own. They require answers. Some people do not live like Jesus is real, because they are not sure He is real. If this is true for you, don't abandon ship on your faith. "Does God exist?" and "Who is Jesus?" are the most important questions you can answer for yourself.

Scrutinize the resources available; those from your church as well as those from this study. Atheist Web sites sometimes say "think for yourself" and "be willing to follow where the evidence leads." I totally agree; but that means being open to the possibility that God's existence is real. If you find Him to be real and true, this conclusion will change your life.

Ask yourself: *Have I been living like God's existence is actually true? What would be evidence one way or the other from my lifestyle?*

In what ways has your life changed because you believe God really exists? Or how might it change if you really did believe?

One of the major changes the reality of God's existence made in my life was in the effect on my emotions. I realized I could not ignore that God was Lord over my emotions. I could no longer use my emotions as an excuse to behave poorly. That leads us to the next category of objections: the emotional objections to belief.

EMOTIONAL OBJECTION: An objection to God generally rooted in some experience of unhappiness in a person's life, which leads to distrust in or disillusionment with God. For example "I stopped believing in God when I was 12 years old and my grandfather died from cancer."

Emotional objections can be deeply troubling. I find them the most difficult obstacles to get past. This roadblock doesn't just require answers, it also requires healing. Emotional roadblocks to faith can result from:

- a hurt caused by a church member;
- distrust of the institutionalized church;
- unrealistic expectations due to bad theology;
- suffering from an injury, disease, or death;
- anger toward God due to life experiences; or
- even pride issues.

Of course, many more can also occur, but these might help bring to mind some of the reasons for the emotional objection to God.

What other emotional reasons can you think of for why people object to belief in God?

With what emotional reasons for rejecting God have you dealt?

How have you gotten past the emotional objections?

When you encounter an emotional objector to God, you may find that the person is not up front with the objection. They may give you an array of intellectual objections in place of the real issue. It may take some time, and some trust, to get a person to reveal an emotional objection. Others may offer it right up front; for example, "I cannot believe in a God who allowed my mom to be killed by a drunk driver when I was just a teenager."

What is the basic objection stated here, and how would you respond to it?

If you know a person whose objection is an emotional resistance to God, pray that God would help them through their suffering. Pray that God would help them to see truth in the midst of even great anguish. And pray for opportunities to both show love and share truth with that person.

It may be difficult to think of a person with an emotional objection if you are not used to looking for emotional versus intellectual objections. Don't give up. Think of the person who will not reason with you and perhaps who gets defensive when it comes to discussion about God.

Think of ways you can help a person with an emotional objection to God. Be ready to share these with your group.

DAY THREE

ROADBLOCK #3: EXPERIENCE

Several years ago, I agreed to participate in my first public, formal debate. Though I had engaged in many online written exchanges, I was nervous about doing a live, in-person debate. I didn't know what to expect since I lacked experience. We may avoid faith conversations because we don't have experience in conversing about beliefs with others.

Today we are going to explore a thought from day 1 a little further: the idea of getting past fear and gaining experience. We know that God commands us to go and tell people about Him (see Matt. 28:19-20), but we may be fearful of the unknown in faith conversations. We can really only get past the fear of the unknown one way—do stuff. We must try it out, making the unknown known.

I grew up near a suburb of Portland, Oregon, called Beaverton. It's also the hometown of the famous athletic-wear company, Nike. In 1988, Nike debuted their new slogan, "Just Do It." This slogan has been named one of the top 5 most influential ad slogans of the 20th century.[3]

The force of the ad message is in part due to the simplicity of the message. You gain experience no other way than to have experiences. Instead of talking about talking about God, we must get out there and just do it.

How does actually engaging in conversation help you get past the fear of the unknown in conversations?

What are other benefits of the "just do it" approach?

Of course, once in a while, you probably will have a bad experience in a conversation with someone. I've found that discussing the worst-case scenario can help women get past the fear of that particular situation. So let's do an example of the worst thing that can happen in a faith conversation.

You hear a person say, "Christianity is for the unintelligent and simple-minded."

You ask them, "What do you mean by that?"

Now a conversation has begun and you quickly see that you are outmatched in wits and in general knowledge about the subject that ensues. What is your fear.

- Are you afraid of looking unintelligent?
- Are you afraid of embarrassment?
- Are you afraid of missing an opportunity to share Jesus? (See Confidence Builder on p. 101.)
- Are you fearful of leading the person further away from truth?

What would be your concern (or fear) about your portion of the above conversation?

What benefits can you think of from having a bad experience in faith conversations?

I have found that, if I'm willing, I can learn from bad experiences. Sometimes I am the one who failed miserably in the conversation or presentation.

Sometimes, it was the other person who failed miserably. In either case, I am growing and learning from these experiences. I'm not saying I don't get hurt by a bad experience but I always have the potential to learn from them. Look again at our theme Scripture 1 Peter 3:15.

What two things does Peter remind the persecuted Christians to do?

How does the reminder to be prepared to make a case apply to your experiences, both past and future?

A few ministry friends and I rotate through a speaker list for a local college ministry. We speak at the student union on various theological, philosophical, and apologetic topics. At one of these events, a pastor friend of mine was speaking on the reasons people doubt God when a philosophy professor in the audience asked him a loaded question on the subject of Hell. The question was where my pastor friend thought well-intentioned Muslims and Jews would go when they died.

The pastor told him that the Bible says that anyone who has not repented of their sins and put their trust in Christ would be separated from God in Hell. My friend had never been confronted in such a way before. He answered politely, yet with conviction. However, at his reply, the professor erupted into a volatile response calling him arrogant and utilizing inappropriate language in front of the audience.

Later, I spoke with my friend about the experience. He said he was glad he had been prepared with a solid foundation in his beliefs. It didn't fluster him when the professor had reacted so aggressively. Plus, instead of hindering him from future conversation, it encouraged my friend by showing him that he was able to handle a worst case in a conversation. Now that he has some experience, he doesn't have that particular fear of the unknown.

Though you may never speak in front of a group like my friend, think about how you would get through a similar aggressive response.

What is the importance of gaining experience in these kinds of situations for you? for those who are observers?

Maybe you've had an experience in evangelism or in conversation that causes you to cringe when you think of discussing your beliefs.

Think of a bad experience you've had talking about your beliefs. Note it here.

As you go back over the situation in your mind, what could you have done better?

What was out of your control?

How will you deal with a similar situation in the future?

CONFIDENCE BUILDER:

You may encounter a question about the existence of Hell when you talk with people about God. Currently, this is a hot topic in popular culture. Here are a couple of things to keep in mind with questions about Hell such as "Do you believe the followers of all other religions are going to Hell?"

1) You should ask the person if they believe in Hell. If they say no, ask why they are asking you a question about something they do not believe in. Look back at the question you were asked; it assumes Hell is real.

2) Find out if they have considered what they believe to be criteria for a person's admittance to Heaven or Hell. So if a person does believe in Hell but still asks, "Do you think everyone who disagrees with you is going to Hell?" You could ask in response, "Do you think anyone goes there? For instance, is Hitler in Hell?" If you get a response like, "Of course Hitler's in Hell," then you can ask, "How do you think God decides who goes to Heaven or Hell?"

3) Try your best to dispel poorly argued sound-bite theology on the doctrine of Hell while graciously engaging the person standing before you. To do so, hold the person accountable to evidence their view of Hell. The Christian doctrine of Hell is rooted in the authority of the person of Jesus Christ and His words about Hell in the New Testament. Remember, if Jesus is God, He has unparalleled authority on this issue. How is the person before you evidencing their view? Are they referencing an authority? Who? Why is the person referenced an authority on the issue?[4]

As my pastor friend mentioned, preparation in our beliefs builds confidence. Nothing can substitute for knowing what you believe and why you believe it. However, nothing will help you to clarify what you believe and why like difficult conversations. Ironically we may even benefit more from what we perceive to be our failures because they can motivate us to dig and improve.

Experiences help you to understand your need to clarify what you believe and why. People ask me all kinds of different questions about my beliefs. Much of what I have learned is a direct result of being asked to support my beliefs or being asked why I believe something is true.

You are going to continue to have experiences with people of different beliefs. It's better to be prepared to learn from these experiences, rather than continue to repeat the problems of bad interactions or let past experiences mentally beat you down.

As the baboon, Rafiki, taught the lion, Simba, in movie, *The Lion King,* the past can hurt, but you can learn from it. You can be prepared for the next time a baboon tries to hit you in the head with a stick.

If you've been verbally abused in the past for your beliefs, what can you do the next time a person tries to do the same thing?

DAY FOUR

BEYOND THE ROADBLOCKS

So far this week, we've looked at three basic roadblocks to conversations.

1) You
2) The objections of others
3) Experience

What other roadblocks to faith conversation do you think you will encounter?

Are there still some roadblocks that you have to faith conversations?

If you are willing, make notes here and plan to discuss with your group the roadblocks that are giving you troubles. Brainstorm ways to get past those remaining blockades.

Today, we will break down the anatomy of a conversation and interact with the various parts. Is this a somewhat clinical approach to the topic? Yes, indeed. I am an apologist after all!

(Day 4 continues on p. 130.)

ANATOMY OF A FAITH CONVERSATION Scenario #1:

First, you hear an objection or snarky comment.

ROADBLOCK #1:
YOU
a. What hang-up might keep you from engaging in conversation?
b. Decide how you are going to deal with your inner hang up and move into conversation.

Second, you are ready with a question. You ask it.
If you never practiced asking your questions from week 4, now's the time!

Third, the person responds.

ROADBLOCK #2:
OBJECTIONS
a. Ask yourself: *Is this an intellectual or emotional objection?*
b. Ask a follow-up question relevant to the roadblock and/or remind them of the original statement if they have trailed off to a new subject.
c. Respond by either:
  i. Engaging in this response.
  ii. Continuing to ask questions for further clarification.
(I typically choose the latter.)

Fourth, you ask another question for further clarification.

Fifth, the person responds.

ROADBLOCK #3:
EXPERIENCE
a. Perhaps this time you are unfamiliar with the material in the response so you may think you should bow out of the conversation.
b. Instead, take this moment as an opportunity to learn from them.

Sixth, you ask a question or respond.

CHOOSE YOUR OWN ADVENTURE:
1. Ask for a thorough explanation of the unfamiliar material.
2. Respond: You are not familiar and would like to read what they have read, getting back with them at a later time.
3. Go back to questioning, such as "Why do you believe this is true?"

Seventh, the person responds or asks you a clarifying question.

Eighth, the conversation continues back and forth until you both decide to wrap it up. Of course, all the way through, you are listening so that you are engaged in actively learning their position and why they believe it is true.

Now let's put this scenario into practice in a mock dialogue! You'll use this material in your group session for practicing out loud with others.

1) Write out one objection you've encountered from a friend or family member (or online or in the media).

2) List the hang-ups that may be a roadblock to engaging in conversation on this objection. Share these with your conversation partner(s).

3) Write how you plan to get past the hang-up. You will tell your conversation partner(s).

4) Write a question you would use in response.

5) What is a possible response to your question? Is this response an intellectual or emotional objection?

6) How are you going to respond? Choose an option below and write out a reply that corresponds with your option.

i. Question

ii. Response

iii. Leave the conversation

7) What would be a response from the other person to your chosen option from question 6?

8) Assume the other person has now shown that they have more background in this subject than you. How are you going to respond?

9) How can you graciously wrap up a conversation?

Congratulations! You made it through a mini mock dialogue! Let's do one more mock dialogue with a different, and more specific, scenario.

ANATOMY OF A FAITH CONVERSATION Scenario #2:

First, you are discussing church with family and a family member makes an objection to or snarky comment about faith.

ROADBLOCK #1:
YOU:
a. Identify a hang-up that might keep you from engaging in conversation.
b. Decide how you are going to respond to yourself in order to move into conversation.

Second, you are ready with a question. You ask it.

Third, the person responds with an obviously emotional objection (not smoke-screened behind intellectual objections).

ROADBLOCK #2:
OBJECTIONS

a. Since this is a family member and their objection is emotional, you must proceed with care.
   i. This is where practicing questions out loud is vital. You and your family members have a "history" and they may perceive your questions differently from what you meant to say.
   ii. Practicing questions in front of others will help you to detect any perception of aggression or defensiveness in your tone (your conversation partners can tell you).
b. Ask a question relevant to the roadblock and/or remind them of the original statement if they have trailed off to a new subject.
c. Choose your own adventure:
   i. Engage in this response.
   ii. Go back to asking questions for further clarification (I typically choose the latter).

Fourth, you ask another question for further clarification.

Fifth, the person responds.

ROADBLOCK #3:
EXPERIENCE

a. Perhaps you don't have experience discussing God with your own family members, and you may resist gaining that experience.
b. Take this as an opportunity to possibly change the dynamic in your family to one of open inquiry about God. Depending on your situation, this will be harder for some and easier for others; either way, it is worth trying.

Sixth, you ask a question or respond.

Seventh, the person responds or asks you a clarifying question.

Eighth, the conversation continues back and forth until either you both decide to wrap it up and/or you detect the family member is getting uncomfortable or defensive.

CONFIDENCE BUILDER: Recognizing Emotional Objections

How can you tell if someone is emotionally objecting to God or if they have a straight-up intellectual objection? Sometimes, discerning an emotional objection can be difficult. A person may have a hurt in the past that they are not sharing with you which relates to their objection to God. They may use intellectual objections as a somewhat of a smoke screen to avoid addressing the actual problem. However, you can detect some obvious emotional objections.

A straight-up intellectual objection doesn't require negative modifiers to make the argument. Look for negatively charged words in the statement that indicate a personal repulsion, disgust, distrust, and dislike. Here are some examples.

"How can you believe in a God so narcissistic that He sends people to Hell for not believing in Him?"

"How about you actually try and provide an argument to support your position, instead of asking your magical sky daddy to brainwash me?"

"You believe in a Jewish zombie."

"Christians want to blind you with their ignorance, saving you from thinking."

"They want to save you from their godboy Jesus, who is going to torture you forever if you don't accept Him as your master."

When you find an obvious emotional objection, you have some options. First, I would address any actual argument aside from all the negative language. I do this frequently in online conversations. Second, you can point out the problematic use of negative language (especially since a logical fallacy is often involved with such language). Third, you can choose to leave a conversation until such a time as the person can argue without being derogatory. Can you think of other options?

Remember, since this is an emotional issue, it may take some time for the wound to heal; in the meantime the person may be a bit callous or lash out.

Do one more complete dialogue set with an emotional objection from a family member. Be ready to do mock dialogues (with responses) this week in group using this material.

A vital aspect of this study is that you engage in conversation with people of different beliefs from your own. Otherwise, this study could end up collecting dust on your shelf, as a Bible study trophy. My hope is that the memories you create of this study come from the new conversations and experiences you will have with others.

Without a doubt, it's the interesting people I have met over the years through faith conversations that keep me coming back for more. Every person has a story about why they are where they are in life and how they came to their current understanding of God. That's what this study is all about: connecting with people in great conversation about God. It's about finding out how the people in your life came to their understanding about God and discussing that story.

It's also about being effective in conversation; even—or especially—with family members. Effectiveness doesn't come from a slick presentation of intellectual zingers. It comes from a person whose conversation is an outworking of loving God and loving others (and by loving God I mean with all our heart, soul, and mind).

Why is it vital that you engage people with different beliefs from your own in conversation?

What role does the actual engagement with opposing viewpoints play in developing you as a good conversationalist?

How is a person's effectiveness in conversation tied to their love of God and love of others?

What does it mean to love God with all your heart, soul, and mind?

DAY FIVE

PUTTING IT ALL TOGETHER

All through this study we've drawn a connection between apologetics, spiritual transformation, and evangelism. The purpose of learning good reasons to believe in God is to build your own faith and is for your own growth: for loving God with all your heart, soul, and mind. After apologetics has washed over our inner being, we can then use the arguments outwardly with others.

How are the areas of apologetics, spiritual transformation, and evangelism connected?

I didn't learn good reasons to believe in God so I could beat people over the head with these truths. I learned the reasons for my own growth and to see change in my own life. Out of that change came a desire to care for others and a confidence in what I believed. These changes have overflowed into all areas of my life; including my relationships with my husband, my daughter, my parents, my friends, and people I meet in the community.

Why do you think apologetics (studying the reasoning for your beliefs) can change a person's relationships?

Do you think it always changes people? Why or why not?

What did the friend's son conclude about his mom's faith?

What can we do to be changed by our study in apologetics as opposed to just gaining an argument to "zing" people?

Why did he come to that conclusion?

I see God as absolutely real and that transformed my perspective on life: I am truly accountable to God for my thoughts and actions toward others. So if I think and behave like a selfish, proud jerk—even if I can quote or teach the Bible—I am not living what is true and good.

I am responsible to God for my thoughts and actions. This move from apologetics as personal transformation to apologetics as evangelism is the way it's going to have to happen if we want to be effective apologists for the Lord.

I read a story by J.P. Moreland several years ago that best illuminated this point for me. A woman who was a friend of Moreland's called him distraught because a large number of non-Christian friends and relatives were regularly asking her hard questions about her faith that she could not answer. One of these questioners was her teenage son. She was concerned that if she couldn't answer him, he wouldn't respect her dedication to Christ. However, her son noted, "She had time to do a number of hobbies, watch television, and so on, so that if getting good answers to certain questions mattered to her, she would have gotten them by now. He concluded that her faith must not matter that much to her, because she had not taken the time to wrestle with issues that might show her faith was false."[5]

Statistics show that 3 out of 5 young adults (59 percent) leave the church once they get out on their own, away from the family.[6] Several reasons are indicated, but one reason not explored yet is the lack of transformation in their parents' lives.

Just as this young man noted, if the parents are not modeling the importance of their beliefs by defending them—or if the parents do not have an understanding of why they believe—they pass this model on to their children. Children can see the discrepancy between theory—Jesus is God and therefore the greatest teacher/thinker who ever lived—and practice—I am committed to learning from the greatest teacher/thinker who ever lived.

How well do you think you put into practice Christian concepts and beliefs (including doctrines of the faith)?

Would your children (or friends and family) say you practice the beliefs of Christianity in your daily living? Why or why not?

We're not just modeling for our children; we're also modeling for our world. Transformation is essential to having a voice in our world. As Christian apologist, Francis Schaeffer, stated, "I believe with all my heart that in order to speak to this generation we must *act* like a Bible-believing people. We can emphasize a message faithful to the Bible and the purity of the visible church, but if we do not practice this truth we cannot expect anyone to listen to us. Yet we must go on even deeper … to a Bible-centered spirituality."[7]

At the beginning of this study we looked at the importance of apologetics to us as individual believers.

List the reasons for apologetics; the ABCs. (If necessary see p. 15.)

A

B

C

Notice that last reason: to change lives … starting with your life. Christians who are transformed are attractive to others who may ask for the reason for the hope that is within them. Jesus says more is at stake in our individual transformation than just what benefits us. Do you remember Francis Schaeffer's "final apologetic" from week 1 (p. 24–25)?

Write the verses here.

Reread these verses.

Write out the final apologetic.

As we go out into our communities, holding people accountable to evidence and reason their own views, we must remember Jesus' words about how the world will judge whether or not He is God's Son. That judgment has a lot to do with our individual attitudes and actions; especially toward each other—including toward our children and family.

· • · •

REVIEW

In wrapping up our time together, let's do a bit of review of the past six weeks.

Week 1

Name one objection to apologetics.

What is your response to this objection?

Name one merit of apologetics.

Week 2

What was one thing you learned in week 2 that you didn't previously know?

Think of an objection with which you might be able to respond using that knowledge. Write it here.

Think of a question you could ask about that objection for further clarification before you respond. Write it here.

Week 3

Write out the verse from Proverbs that most impacted you.

Who is "the fool" according to the proverbs we studied?

How are you going to guard against building straw men when discussing other people's views?

Why is it important to represent others' ideas accurately?

What are some physical ways you can listen better?

Week 4

What are some questions you can ask a person for further clarification?

How do you get back on track when a person keeps changing the subject or presents an unrelated argument?

Week 5

What challenges do you foresee you will have in offering responses to people who have objections to God?

Do you need to have all the answers to begin talking with people about belief in God?

Name one way to demonstrate honesty in our conversations with others.

Remember that we aren't just out telling people what is "true for us." We are sharing what we believe is true. Period. That is a tough calling at times.

Throughout history, people have rejected the actual truth for an untruth of their own making (see Isa. 59:14). It has always been difficult to share truth with a person who doesn't want truth. Who is that person? The person who wants truth to be whatever works for them. I have found that even people who call themselves freethinkers can be enslaved to their own presuppositions, unwilling to go where the evidence leads.

So you have your work cut out for you. It is worth it. You are needed in the battle for truth.

This is not the work for "others" with a gift or calling. It is the work of the body of Christ: to bring truth, which is light, to mankind. We cannot afford to view this work as a luxury; lives are at stake. So choose with whom you will begin. Who will you ask for the first time, "Why do you believe that?"

YOU ARE THE LIGHT OF THE WORLD. A CITY SET ON A HILL CANNOT BE HIDDEN. NOR DO PEOPLE LIGHT A LAMP AND PUT IT UNDER A BASKET, BUT ON A STAND, AND IT GIVES LIGHT TO ALL IN THE HOUSE. IN THE SAME WAY, LET YOUR LIGHT SHINE BEFORE OTHERS, SO THAT THEY MAY SEE YOUR GOOD WORKS AND GIVE GLORY TO YOUR FATHER WHO IS IN HEAVEN. MATTHEW 5:14-16

GROUP

What are some of the issues that make conversations difficult for you?

What benefits can come from having a bad experience in faith conversations?

What roadblocks continue to give you trouble? What ways might you get past those roadblocks?

In reviewing our time together, what has been most helpful?

On what area do you most need to continue to work?

VIDEO GUIDE

Your spirited _____ is desperately needed today in our culture.

We engage in this battle of the mind for our own _____.

The best way for you to begin is to get out there and let people _____ _____ _____.

LEADER
GUIDE

Thank you for leading a group to equip believers in the critical field of apologetics through this study *Why Do You Believe That?* I pray that God will reward your hard work in ways that only eternity will be able to fully express. In this leader guide you will find several elements.

For initial promotion and ongoing encouragement to members, I have included suggested entries for use in social media, e-mail, and church bulletins. Think creatively about how you can encourage women to participate and to remain faithful.

The session suggestions provide for seven group sessions. You can do the study with group sessions from 1–2 hours. Ideally you would benefit from having at least 1½ hours. In session 1, you will get acquainted, distribute member books, and view session 1 video. In the later sessions, you will be talking about the previous week's homework before viewing the 20–27 minute video segments.

You will find leader suggestions in this section, but the group sessions are designed for members to complete and discuss the group and viewer guide pages that accompany each week's homework. The group page provides discussion questions for the session. Supplement these with the suggestions in the leader guide.

Because every group is different, I have sought to provide you several sample discussion suggestions, likely more than your group will be able to use. Do not feel that you must cover all of these suggestions and activities. They serve as only a guide. You know your group best. Prayerfully choose those learning activities that may be most helpful to your group. Remember that in all faith conversations flexibility and dependence on the Holy Spirit are paramount.

Your role as group leader will mean far more by encouraging discovery than by teaching the content. Do not feel that you must be an expert. We're all on the learning journey together here.

Keep in mind that the real purpose of the group is to equip believers with conversation skills. The group will be successful to the degree that members wind up having good conversations with those outside the faith. Therefore plan your lesson strategy with that goal in mind. You may choose to spend group-session time processing the questions from your member books, or you may choose to develop your own lesson-plan strategy. The important question is: what will help you and your group members to develop the skill set and knowledge necessary to become more effective conversationalists?

PROMOTING THE GROUP

Every believer needs the subject matter in *Why Do You Believe That?* Unfortunately, just as we don't automatically want to eat or exercise like we should, most of us have to be encouraged to confront our fears and learn to defend our faith. Pray about how you can encourage participation in this study. Nothing takes the place of personal invitation. Use church bulletins, announcements in Bible study classes, and church services. Additionally, here are some suggested social media announcements.

FACEBOOK AND TWITTER UPDATES

Starting a brand new 7-session study to help us gain confidence in discussing belief in God! Mon. 8/20 @7pm in Rm. 113

Why Do You Believe That? Join us for an upcoming Bible study on confident & effective conversations about belief in God. Mon. 8/20 @7pm in Rm. 113

Join us for a 7-session women's Bible study in apologetics! Answer your doubts. Build your confidence. Start changing lives. Mon. 8/20 @7pm in Rm. 113

CHURCH BULLETIN ANNOUNCEMENT

Why Do You Believe That? A Faith Conversation Bible study

How confident do you feel in talking about matters of faith? Do you wish you could express your beliefs with more effectiveness? Join us in a practical 7-session study to gain understanding and skill in sharing Jesus effectively with others and in better understanding your own faith. Answer your doubts. Build your confidence. Start changing lives.

The learning begins Mon. 8/20 @7pm in Rm. 113. Contact _____ for more information.

PINTEREST

Promotional *Why Do You Believe That?* images available for pinning at *www.pinterest.com/lifewaywomen*

· · · · ·

SESSION ONE: (INTRODUCTION TO STUDY) INTRODUCTION TO APOLOGETICS

BEFORE THE SESSION

1. Pray for those who will participate.
2. Preview session 1 video and look over your member book. Prepare to point out the components, requirements, and benefits of the study.

FACEBOOK AND TWITTER UPDATES

WDYBT? Wk 1: This week we'll study why we should be able to give the reasons for our faith in God. Mon. 8/20 @7pm in Rm. 113

WDYBT? Wk 1: Do you know people who doubt God's existence or have trouble trusting Him? Come to group session 1. Mon. 8/20 @7pm in Rm. 113

E-MAIL

Hey (friends, ladies, crew, classmates),

I'm looking forward to our first session together. We'll dig into why Christians need to know how to make a case for their beliefs (apologetics). We'll also discover what is apologetics and discuss some of the merits and objections of studying apologetics. Most importantly, we will begin the process of answering our own doubts to build confidence for our conversations about belief in God.

I can't wait to get started. See you Mon. 8/20 @7pm in Rm. 113!

For more information on our study check out: *www.lifeway.com/maryjosharp*

For more information on our author check out her blog: *www.maryjosharp.com*

PINTEREST

Promotional *Why Do You Believe That?* images available for pinning at *www.pinterest.com/lifewaywomen*

DURING THE SESSION
....

INTRODUCTION

Greet group members as they arrive. Lead a get-acquainted activity such as everyone answering the following questions about themselves.

1. Where were you born, and what was your family like?
2. How long have you lived in your present home, and who shares it with you?
3. What difference do you think it would make in your life if you felt really comfortable sharing your faith with others?

Explain that this study will seek to provide a balance of two areas:

1. training in developing the skills to be a good conversationalist; and
2. learning information to effectively share and defend their faith.

DISCUSSION

Discuss the following with your group.

1. Why do you think both training and learning are important?
2. What happens to our attempts to share our faith if either is lacking?
3. Do we tend to take either for granted?

Direct members to the introduction on pages 6–7. Take a few minutes to discuss the introduction. Encourage members to put in the effort necessary to get the most from the study.

WATCH

1. Watch session 1 video. Direct members to complete the viewer guide on page 11.
2. Ask group members the following questions in response to the video.

- What issue most stands out to you from the video and/or the group discussion?
- What would you like to set as a personal goal for this study?

Encourage members the assignments in their member books. Pray and dismiss.

SESSION TWO: (WEEK 1 HOMEWORK) KNOWING YOUR BELIEFS

BEFORE THE SESSION

1. Pray for your group members.
2. Complete week 1 homework and preview the session 2 video.
3. On a whiteboard or tear sheet, write separately the following two statements.
   • Objective: to understand the concept of apologetics and to value becoming an effective apologist
   • Bill Maher: "Faith is a lack of critical thinking."
4. Get a tool belt or tool kit to use as a visual aid for the "building a conversation" segments—the more outlandish the better. Plan to use the tool kit as an ongoing visual aid for your study. Prepare to lead a discussion of the elements of a good conversation. For this week you might just show the entire kit as "elements of a good conversation." Then for subsequent weeks use tool ideas of your own. Exercise your creativity and have fun with this. Possibilities might include the following.
   • Session 2 elements of conversation: the entire tool kit or tool belt
   • Session 3 know: a how-to book, set of plans, dress pattern, or a table of sizes of some item (nails, nuts and bolts, etc.)
   • Session 4 listening: stethoscope, phone, piece of hose (for listening for location of a noise in an engine), or a baby monitor
   • Session 5 questions: plumb line, level, scale, or any diagnostic instrument
   • Session 6 responding: megaphone, tape measure, repair manual, or telephone
   • Session 7 roadblocks: hammer or battering ram, wrecking bar, saw, or something that suggests overcoming obstacles

FACEBOOK AND TWITTER UPDATES

WDYBT? Wk 2: What would you say if you were asked, "Why do you believe in God?" Join us this week: Mon. 8/20 @7pm in Rm. 113

Got a minute? Watch this: _____
Then join us for wk 2 of "Why Do You Believe That?" Mon. 8/20 @7pm in Rm. 113

Troubled that you won't be able to answer the question, "Why do you believe in God?" Join us: Mon. 8/20 @7pm in Rm. 113

E-MAIL

Hey (friends, ladies, crew, classmates),

Our last session together was great! Next week we're digging into some of the tough questions of our faith. We'll also discover how knowing what you believe can help you in conversations with others.

BECAUSE THE MATERIAL on the Internet is constantly changing, we have not recommended specific links. If you will search on the Internet, you will find an enormous number of attacks on belief in God and on Christianity. As you develop your lesson plans, you might consider asking members to respond to some of the clips you will find. Be aware that many of the attacks are profane and vile, but that is the world Jesus calls us to engage with His message of redemption.

I look forward to seeing you there! See you Mon. 8/20 @7pm in Rm. 113!

PINTEREST

Promotional *Why Do You Believe That?* images available for pinning at *www.pinterest.com/lifewaywomen*

DURING THE SESSION

1. Welcome group members as they arrive.
2. Point out the objective for the session.
3. Lead the group to pray for objective.

INTRODUCTION

As a group, process your choice of the following questions and topics. Each time someone responds, try to give her positive feedback, even if all you can say is "thank you" with a smile. Positive feedback will help encourage future interaction. Remember that the purpose of the group is to develop conversation skills. People need to express their ideas verbally to overcome fears and practice engaging others in conversation.

Direct them to the Bill Maher comment from *The View*. Ask:

- Is this really what belief in God is all about? Is faith just wishful thinking or a silly whim? Why or why not?
- How would you respond to Maher?

Explain: "Beliefs aren't true because we believe them. They are true when they match up with the reality of the universe in which we live. We shouldn't believe in God simply because it makes us feel good, because we just want it to be true, or because that's what we've always believed. We are supposed to discover why we believe something is true and then continue to learn about our beliefs to gain confidence. Bill Maher makes belief in God look ridiculous, rather than reasoned; as if there are no good reasons to believe in God. But once we know why we believe something to be true, it doesn't make sense to be embarrassed about our reasoned beliefs. Maher's example is one of extreme unreasonableness toward persons of religious faith. This is divisive behavior instead of reasonable argument."

Explain that we want to learn how to better engage others in discussion on beliefs. This starts with building a strong foundation of what we believe.

Show the group your tool belt or tool kit labeled "conversation." Say: "Each week we will add a new tool to our conversation kit. When we finish we will have the tools to have more productive and effective conversations about faith. This week's tool is conversation."

Hold up the tool representing or labeled "conversation" and place it in the kit.

DISCUSSION QUESTIONS FROM WEEK 1

Choose the questions from week 1 that stood out to you to highlight and discuss. Plan for about 5 minutes or so of discussion on each question. Remember to allow class members to do most of the talking. Keep in mind that a major goal of this study is to get members talking about their beliefs. You may choose to ask what part of the lesson really impacted them this week and simply guide the discussion.

- What change in your life, relationships, and self confidence do you think being better able to make a case for your faith would make? (p. 13)
- What reasons for doubt about God's existence have you heard? (p. 15)
- What changes do you think defending our beliefs can have on our lives and why? (p. 18)
- What have you identified that you can do differently in conversations to avoid anger while discussing beliefs? (p. 20)

- Describe an objection to Christianity and one question you could ask about that objection that might lead to further understanding (p. 22).
- How can we help a person who has an emotional objection to God? (p. 23)
- What additional reasons for studying apologetics did you identify? (p. 24)
- What do you think are the differences between good arguing and bad arguing? (p. 24)
- Why do you think the "final apologetic" is important? (p. 25)

WATCH

1. Introduce next week's material by showing the session 2 video.
2. After the video, briefly wrap up. Thank participants for their work. Encourage them for the week to come.

DURING THE WEEK

- Call any members who may be particularly struggling or just to give encouragement.
- Make announcements and updates through social media.

· · · · ·

SESSION THREE: (WEEK 2 HOMEWORK) LISTENING TO OTHERS

BEFORE THE SESSION

1. Pray for each group member by name.
2. Complete week 2 homework and preview session 3 video.
3. Prepare tool kit or tool belt for visual aid with tool labeled "know" or "know what you believe."
4. Use social media suggestions or your own ideas during the week to promote and encourage faithfulness.

FACEBOOK AND TWITTER UPDATES

WDYBT? Wk 3: How well do you listen to the arguments of others? Join us this week: Mon. 8/20 @7pm in Rm. 113

Listening to minister. Listening to spread truth. Join us for wk 3 of "Why Do You Believe That?" Mon. 8/20 @7pm in Rm. 113

Listening is a means of accountability. Join us: Mon. 8/20 @7pm in Rm. 113

E-MAIL

Hey (friends, ladies, crew, classmates),

We had a great time of learning in week 2! Thanks for being a part of the great conversation. If you missed us, don't worry. Come on and join us next week as we delve into one of the most understated aspects of good conversation: the ability to listen well. I think you'll enjoy a different perspective on how listening can change your conversations about God.

See you Mon. 8/20 @7pm in Rm. 113!

PINTEREST

Promotional *Why Do You Believe That?* images available for pinning at *www.pinterest.com/lifewaywomen*

DURING THE SESSION

1. Welcome group members as they arrive.
2. Point out the objective for the session.
3. Lead the group to pray for objective to know what we believe so we can be effective in conversation.
4. Use the visual tool.

INTRODUCTION

Say: "Each week we're adding a new tool to our conversation kit. This week's tool is knowing what you believe." Hold up the tool representing or labeled "know" and place it in the kit.

Explain: "When we know what we believe and why we believe it, we build confidence in our beliefs. That confidence helps us to better express our beliefs and helps us to better engage with people of different beliefs."

DISCUSSION QUESTIONS FROM WEEK 2

Choose questions from week 2 you would like to highlight and discuss. Suggested questions include:

- Why do you think knowing what you believe about God is essential to having good conversations with others about God? (p. 30)
- How would you respond to the statement that for Christians to say that Jesus is the only way is intolerant? (p. 31)
- How do you define tolerance? (p. 31)
- How could you explain to a person who thinks you are intolerant that Christianity is actually a very tolerant religion? (p. 33)
- Why is it important when having faith conversations to know how our basic beliefs differ from other religions and views? (p. 35)
- How can we convey an attitude of loving what is true and loving all people? (p. 38)
- How would you explain to a new believer the crucial nature of the resurrection of Jesus? (p. 38)

- How would you explain to an interested unbeliever how you discovered why you believe the resurrection is an historical fact? (p. 39)
- Why do we need to establish the reliability of the text of Scripture before we can claim the inspiration of the contents of Scripture? (p. 45)
- What would you say to a person who told you that we don't know the content of the original New Testament texts? (p. 46)
- What could you say if a person says you cannot trust the Bible since it was written so many years ago? (p. 46)

Statement/Response Option

Present some wrong statements about the Christian faith and have your group give responses to the statement. These go along with days from week 2.

Day 1:
- Christians are intolerant of other views.

Day 2:
- All religions teach the same basic ideas.
- Christians think they have the only truth, but that's just arrogant. All religions are equally true for whoever believes them.
- Stop forcing your religious views on me!

Day 3:
- Jesus wasn't really raised from the dead. That's just a myth.

Day 4:
- Christians don't think for themselves.
- Religion teaches people what to think, not how to think.

Day 5:
- You cannot trust the Bible. It has been changed over the years.
- You cannot trust the Bible. A bunch of men put it together two thousand years ago.

Subgroup Activity Option

Have the group break up into small groups to practice discussing wrong views of the Christian faith. Individuals should think of more objections they have heard that do not aptly represent Christianity. (Please make a note to group: These are not to be "in-house" theological arguments between Christian views. These are specifically to be incorrect views from outside the Christian faith).

Ask the groups to share any particularly good responses they heard from each other (winsome and constructive responses) and any questions they encountered while studying.

WATCH

1. Watch session 3 video.
2. After the video, briefly wrap up with the following assignment.

Assignment

Say: "This week listen for an opportunity to help someone else better understand the Christian faith. Pray for God to put a person in your path that will challenge your beliefs; specifically in one of the areas we've studied."

Encourage the members that the only way to get better at having conversations is to actually begin to have them. Tell them that next week you want them to share any conversations they have had, whether long or short.

Activities to Engage the Community

Consider these ideas for activities to help your group actively engage in the community.

For small groups:

1. Organize an outing with your church (involving your group as well) to a local coffee shop, bookstore, university event, or any local place at which there will be people of different beliefs, not

a church. This activity can be part of an existing church outreach program, mission trip, special event, or designed specifically for this study.

2. Create a sign, T-shirt, or booth that says, "What do you think about Christianity?" Be sure you contact a manager or the person in charge of the store or event to get approval for your presence if you will be at a private business. Some other ideas for signs are: "Who do you believe Jesus was?" or "If you could ask God one question, what would it be?"

3. Tell your group that you will not be debating people. You will simply survey this week to get a better understanding of different views.

   • Sample dialogue: "I am Mary Jo Sharp from _____ Church. We are attempting to understand better our community's view on God and specifically the view of the Christian faith [or 'the view of God' or 'the view of Jesus']. Would you be willing to provide a quick response to this question? I'm just going to take some notes, but that's really all I'm here to do." *(The person answers and you take notes.)* "So let me see if I understand your view correctly." *(Repeat back to them what they stated and make adjustments for any corrections.)* "Great, thank you so much for your time!"

4. Have the group report back to you the next week with their results. Discuss the varying views and how they differ from what you learned in week 2.

For larger groups:

1. Tell your group that the goal is not to debate people. You will simply survey this week to get a better understanding of different views.

2. Ask an individual you know, "What do you think about Christianity?"

   • Sample dialogue: "I am participating in a study at my church. We are attempting to understand better our community's view on God and spe-

cifically the view of the Christian faith [or 'the view of God' or 'the view of Jesus']. Would you be willing to provide a quick response to this question? I'm just going to take some notes, but that's really all I'm going to do." *(The person answers and you take notes.)* "So let me see if I understand your view correctly." *(Repeat back to them what they stated and make adjustments for any corrections.)* "Great, thank you so much! This is helpful."

3. Have the group report back to you the next week with their results. Discuss the varying views and how they differ from what you learned in week 2.

* * * * *

SESSION FOUR: (WEEK 3 HOMEWORK) QUESTIONING OTHERS

BEFORE THE SESSION

1. Pray for each group member by name.
2. Complete week 3 homework and preview session 4 video.
3. Prepare tool kit or tool belt for visual aid with tool labeled "listening."

FACEBOOK AND TWITTER UPDATES

WDYBT? Wk 4: Everyone has a view of the world. All we have to do is ask. Join us this week: Mon. 8/20 @7pm in Rm. 113

Ask questions to better engage in dialogue. Join us for wk 4 of "Why Do You Believe That?" Mon. 8/20 @7pm in Rm. 113

Questioning helps us discover how to better minister to a person. Join us: Mon. 8/20 @7pm in Rm. 113

E-MAIL

Hey (friends, ladies, crew, classmates),

We have the great privilege of asking questions to find out what other people believe and why they believe it. As you'll see in week 4, we're not the only ones with a belief about God. When we ask questions, we discover how to better minister to a person right where they are at in life.

See you Mon. 8/20 @7pm in Rm. 113!

PINTEREST

Promotional *Why Do You Believe That?* images available for pinning at *www.pinterest.com/lifewaywomen*

DURING THE SESSION

1. Welcome group members as they arrive.
2. Point out the objective for the session is to sharpen our listening skills in conversations.
3. Pray for the session and the effectiveness of the training process.

INTRODUCTION

Play Listening Game

Explain: "Let's begin today with a bit of a game. I'm going to begin a story, and you are going to keep it going throughout the room. I'll begin the story and hand it off to someone else. That person will repeat what I said and add a short piece to the story. This will continue on through the group."

Start a story with something like "There once was a girl" Someone in your group repeats the sentence and completes it as in: "There once was a girl named Sandra, who went to the store." The challenge is to listen carefully and to repeat the story up to the point where it left off. As the story winds around and gets outrageous, it becomes more challenging and fun.

Perhaps offer a prize for the person who can repeat correctly most of the story. A great prize would be a book such as *The Fallacy Detective* by Hans and Nathaniel Bluedorn or *Tactics* by Gregory Koukl.

Discuss briefly why the game became more difficult as it went on (emphasize listening and memory).

Show the class the "conversation" tool belt or tool kit. Say: "Each week we're adding a new tool to our conversation kit." Hold up the tool representing or labeled "listening" and place it in the kit.

Explain: "Today we are adding one of the most important and often overlooked tools to effective faith conversations; the ability to listen well. Part of our ministry to others is to hear them out so we can better engage in their actual concerns about God.

DISCUSSION QUESTIONS FROM WEEK 3

Choose questions from week 3 you would like to highlight and discuss. Choose fewer questions than the other weeks if you choose the Errors in Reasoning option; it will require 15–20 minutes. You may choose to discuss the reasoning errors in brief in class and go over them in an online format in detail.

- Why do you think we feel that we have to offer something every time we are with other people? (p. 53)
- How does willingness to listen show love? (p. 54)
- How does our tendency to be unwilling to listen relate to what Proverbs says about being wise or foolish? (pp. 55–57)
- What are some steps we can take to become better able to receive correction? (p. 57)
- What problems can we expect if we are unwilling to have our beliefs corrected or criticized? (p. 58)
- Can you think of and explain some examples of people building straw men? What is wrong with the straw-man approach? (pp. 58–60)
- Have you ever answered a person before you really listened? If so, what was the result? (p. 61)
- How is listening to find points of communication different than listening to argue? (p. 62)
- Do you tend to react defensively when your beliefs are challenged? What can you do if you find yourself responding with defensiveness? (p. 66)
- Share your examples of each error in reasoning. (p. 66)
- What is one thing about listening that you learned this week? (p. 67)
- Discuss the do's and don'ts of good listening. (pp. 67–68)

"Errors in Reasoning" Option (pp. 64–65)

Say: "One of the most vital parts of engaging in productive conversation is to engage in good reasoning. We should help others understand when they have made an error in reasoning, as well as keep ourselves accountable to avoid errors in reasoning. These errors lead us away from truth, not toward it."

Be sure to include the examples of each fallacy. Ask for questions on any of the fallacies.

WATCH

1. Watch session 4 video.
2. After the video, briefly wrap up with the following assignment.

Assignment

Say: "This week we are practicing listening to others. Invite a person who you know disagrees with you on an issue to explain their view on that issue as fully as possible in the amount of time you have with them. Do not interrupt them. Repeat their statements back to them for understanding. Ask questions for clarification on any point. When you have finished your discussion see if you can remember and write down their major points. Write down what you learned from them that you didn't previously know; either about them personally, their view, or the issue in general. This assignment must be completed with a person who is adamantly opposed to you on some issue: political, religious, or so forth. Do not choose a mean or belligerent person for this exercise."

Warn your members to use caution in their choice of person. We do not wish to put them in verbally abusive situations. Tell them that next week you want them to share anything they learned while actively listening and to discuss the experience in general.

Actively Engage in the Community

Host a booth at an event with a sign that says, "Christians who listen. We want to know your concerns about belief in God."

• • • • •

SESSION FIVE: (WEEK 4 HOMEWORK) RESPONDING TO OTHERS

BEFORE THE SESSION

1. Pray for each group member by name.
2. Complete week 4 homework and preview session 5 video. Determine your objective for the week in your own words.
3. Prepare tool kit or tool belt for visual aid with tool labeled "questions" or "asking questions."

FACEBOOK AND TWITTER UPDATES

WDYBT? Wk 5: How well do you respond to a person who has opposing views to your own? Join us Mon. 8/20 @7pm in Rm. 113

Learn how to better respond when faced with questions about your faith. Join us for wk 5 of "Why Do You Believe That?" Mon. 8/20 @7pm in Rm. 113

Respond to a skeptical culture with gentleness and respect. Join us: Mon. 8/20 @7pm in Rm. 113

E-MAIL

Hey (friends, ladies, crew, classmates),

Sometimes it can be a challenge in our current culture to provide an answer for the hope that is in us with gentleness and respect (see 1 Pet. 3:15). However, this is exactly the attitude that Peter has called us to demonstrate when giving a response. This week's lesson will help you discover how to better respond to questions and/or comments about the Christian faith. We'll also continue to practice our conversations!

See you Mon. 8/20 @7pm in Rm. 113!

PINTEREST

Promotional *Why Do You Believe That?* images available for pinning at *www.pinterest.com/lifewaywomen*

DURING THE SESSION:

1. Welcome group members as they arrive.
2. Point out your objective for the session. Invite members to state their objective from their study this week.
3. Call for reports on last week's class assignment on listening. Discuss what they learned and any difficulty they had simply listening without commenting.
4. Pray for objectives and focus of the session.

INTRODUCTION TO DISCUSSION

Watch the classic Abbott and Costello comedy routine, "Who's on First?" See the leader kit video bonus section or find it online.

Explain: "Sometimes our conversations about God can almost be as confusing as the lines in this old comedy routine. But unlike the fun confusion created by Abbott and Costello's questions, the questions we learned this week are intended to help us, as well as the people with whom we speak, better understand individual beliefs about God."

Show the class the tool belt or tool kit. Hold up the tool representing or labeled "question" and place it in the kit.

Explain: "Today we are adding the tool of questions. We should always be ready to ask a few questions about a person's view before we begin to answer them. This is not a trick or an attempt to win an argument. It is a tool to help us clarify the content of a profitable conversation."

Ask your group what part of the lesson really impacted them this week and why it was impacting.
Ask your group for any questions they encountered while studying

DISCUSSION QUESTIONS FROM WEEK 4

Choose those questions from week 4 that you would like to highlight and discuss.

- Have you encountered a person who was making a poor argument against the Christian faith? What was their argument, and how did you respond? (p. 75)
- How would you respond to the theory that a person cannot know truth about God until they get beyond their thinking abilities? (p. 77)
- How would you explain to a friend the idea of a self-defeating statement? (p. 77)
- What are your thoughts about how far we go in a conversation before we walk away? (p. 80)
- What are some benefits of asking "What do you mean by that?" (p. 81)
- What are some benefits of asking "How do you know that?" (p. 82)
- In your own words, what is the difference between asking "How do you know that?" and "Why do you believe that?" (p. 85)
- What could you say to a person who is apathetic about their reasons for belief or disbelief? When a person says that they don't care sometimes they just need a little help to see that they actually do care. One way to demonstrate this is to discuss a political or moral issue you know is meaningful to the person. Most people have a view on emotionally charged issues. Utilizing these issues to show a person that they do care and do have a belief can help move past the apathy. Just be cautious not to divert into a long debate on both your views on that issue. The important part is to get to why they believe their view is the correct one. This can lead back to a conversation on God. For example, What is the standard of good by which they are judging that their view is good? Christians have God as a standard of goodness. You want to direct them back to understanding that their views are formed on their beliefs about God and about the universe. They aren't really apathetic (p. 85).
- Using ideas you've heard from your own interactions with people, what are some ways of softening our questions? (p. 87)
- What are some questions you determined to ask of the statements listed in day 5? (pp. 88–89)

Practice in Pairs or Small Groups

Break into pairs or small groups to actively practice questioning. Use scenarios in the study, or use examples encountered in their own lives.

WATCH

1. Watch session 5 video.
2. After the video, wrap up with the assignment.

Assignment

This week we are practicing our questioning skills. Your assignment this week is to use one or more of these questions in a conversation with a person who disagrees with your belief in God. Remember that you must be asking the question out of a true desire to better understand the person's position.

Also remember that if you are caught in a situation in which you do not know the answer, you should say that you do not know. Phrases you should keep on hand could include:

- "That's a good question, or "That's an interesting thought."
- "I haven't considered that yet. Could you suggest a source for me to look into that argument and I'll get back to you?"
- "Could you explain your view to me so that I can understand it better?"

Tell the group that you want them to share their experience with the group next week.

• • • •

SESSION SIX: (WEEK 5 HOMEWORK) ROADBLOCKS

BEFORE THE SESSION

1. Pray for teach group member by name.
2. Complete week 5 homework and preview session 6 video. Determine your objective for the week in your own words.
3. Prepare your tool kit or tool belt for visual aid with tool labeled "responding."

Show the tool belt or tool kit. Hold up the tool representing or labeled "responding" and place it in the kit. Explain that in learning this week to respond to others, we need to be ready, available, honest, discerning, and prepared.

FACEBOOK AND TWITTER UPDATES

WDYBT? Wk 6: It's time to commence the conversation! Join us Mon. 8/20 @7pm in Rm. 113

Learn the anatomy of a faith conversation. Join us for wk 6 of "Why Do You Believe That?" Mon. 8/20 @7pm in Rm. 113

Do you find there are roadblocks to conversation about faith? Join us: Mon. 8/20 @7pm in Rm. 113

E-MAIL

Hey (friends, ladies, crew, classmates),

We can face a lot of roadblocks to good faith conversation. Sometimes the roadblocks come from others, but sometimes we are the source of the roadblock! This week we'll look at getting beyond the roadblocks so that we can begin having those great conversations.

We'll also discover the difference between an intellectual objection and an emotional objection. Sometimes emotional objections are hidden behind a seemingly intellectual objection. Week 6 helps us to discover these two basic kinds of objections, so we can rightly handle each one.

See you Mon. 8/20 @7pm in Rm. 113!

PINTEREST

Promotional *Why Do You Believe That?* images available for pinning at *www.pinterest.com/lifewaywomen*

INTRODUCTION

Watch "Religious Antagonist." See the DVD kit leader materials or find it online.

Ask the following questions in response to the clip.
- What do you see going on here that is problematic on both sides?
- Are either of the Christians handling this situation of antagonism well? Why or why not?
- What would you do differently in this situation?

Show the class the tool belt or toolkit. Hold up the tool representing or labeled "question" and place it in the kit.

Explain: "Today we are adding the tool of questions. We should always be ready to ask a few questions about a person's view before we begin to answer them."

DISCUSSION QUESTIONS FROM WEEK 5

Choose questions from week 5 you would like to highlight and discuss.
- How would you respond to someone who said something like "You're being illogical"? (p. 98)
- What is the error in the genetic fallacy? What are some examples of where you have heard this reasoning error in use? (p. 98)
- What can you do now to be ready to respond to people who are making poor arguments? (p. 99)
- What example did you write of how to point out errors in reasoning without coming across as disrespectful or angry? (p. 99)

- Have you ever thought of yourself as not good enough to talk to someone about God? Why or why not? (p. 100)
- What can you do to get past an instance when you didn't do well in a conversation? Discuss the value of actually celebrating our failures because they encourage us to learn and grow. We also never know what the Holy Spirit will do with our perceived failures. Our "failures" may often bring more benefit than what we perceive as successes. (p. 100)
- What are some ways we can lose a person's trust in a conversation? (p. 102)
- What are the dangers of treating others as if they were projects? (p. 102)
- What steps might we take to become more willing to admit our errors? (p. 105)
- What do Jesus' words in Matthew 7:16 teach us to do in each circumstance we face? (p. 106)
- If a person doesn't believe the Bible, why might Scriptural reproofs be ineffective? What might be a better course? (p. 106)
- Why should you expect the other person to interact with your views? (p. 108)
- What are some ways you can get back on topic if a person is not interacting with your part of a discussion? (p. 108)
- What are some ways you can continue to humbly serve those who are unready or unwilling to have an honest conversation? (p. 109)
- Which of the quick responses do you relate to most and plan to retain? (pp. 109–111)

WATCH

1. Watch session 6 video.
2. After the video, encourage group members to both practice with other believers and pray for opportunities to have good conversations.

• • • • •

SESSION SEVEN: (WEEK 6 HOMEWORK) WRAP UP & CONCLUSION

BEFORE THE SESSION

1. Pray for each group member by name.
2. Complete week 6 homework and preview the session 7 video. Determine your objective for the week in your own words.
3. Prepare your tool kit or tool belt for visual aid with tool labeled "roadblocks."

FACEBOOK AND TWITTER UPDATES

WDYBT? Wk 7: It's our last session together! See you there: Mon. 8/20 @7pm in Rm. 113

Come hear a final encouraging word from MJ. Join us for wk 7 of "Why Do You Believe That?" Mon. 8/20 @7pm in Rm. 113

Ladies, it's time for us to be "more spirited than lions"! Join us: Mon. 8/20 @7pm in Rm. 113

E-MAIL

Hey (friends, ladies, crew, classmates),

As we come to the close of *Why Do You Believe That?* I want to encourage you to bring one story about how this study has changed your perspective on conversation with others. Perhaps you have a story about a great faith conversation you've had so far. Bring your stories/thoughts/discoveries to our last session together. Let's make this a time of encouragement and commissioning.

See you Mon. 8/20 @7pm in Rm. 113!

PINTEREST

Promotional *Why Do You Believe That?* images available for pinning at *www.pinterest.com/lifewaywomen*

DURING THE SESSION

1. Welcome group members as they arrive.
2. Point out that the objective for the session is to identify and begin to overcome the roadblocks that prevent our engaging in productive conversations. Invite members to state the particular roadblock they would like to overcome or their objective for this final week of the group.

INTRODUCTION

Show the tool belt or tool kit. Explain that this week you are striving together to identify roadblocks to our conversations. Hold up the tool representing or labeled "overcome roadblocks" and place it in the tool kit or belt.

DISCUSSION QUESTIONS FROM WEEK 6

- What are some of the issues that make conversations difficult for you? Why do you think these things keep you from conversing with others? (p. 116)
- What did you identify that you can do to get yourself past some of these hang-ups? (p. 117)
- What is something you hadn't been able to answer in the past but that now you can answer about your faith? (p. 118)
- What is your definition of an intellectual objection to the existence of God? (p. 118)
- When a person doesn't know the source of their objection to the faith, what do you think we can do to help? How might clarifying someone's objection be more helpful than giving answers? (p. 120)
- What emotional reasons can you think of for why people object to belief in God? (p. 121)
- What ways did you think of to help a person with an emotional objection to God? (p. 122)
- How does actually engaging in conversations help you get past the fear of the unknown in conversations? (p. 122)

- What other benefits did you identify for the "just do it" approach? (p. 123)
- What benefits can come from having a bad experience in faith conversations? (p. 123)
- Thinking of a bad experience in a conversation, what could you have done better? What was out of your control? How might you deal with a similar situation in the future? (p. 124)
- What options do you have when you are verbally abused for your beliefs? (p. 125)
- What roadblocks continue to give you trouble? What ways might you get past those roadblocks? (p. 125)
- Why is it vital that we engage in conversation with people of different beliefs from our own? (p. 131)
- What role does the actual engagement with opposing viewpoints play in developing you as a good conversationalist? (p. 131)
- How do you think the areas of apologetics, spiritual transformation, and evangelism are connected? (p. 131)
- What can we do to be changed by our study in apologetics as opposed to just gaining an argument to "zing" people? (p. 132)
- In reviewing our time together, what has been most helpful? On what area do you most need to continue to work? (pp. 133–135)

WATCH

1. Watch session 7 video.
2. We thank you for leading this group in the vital topic of apologetics. You may want to celebrate with a meal or outing with your group. You may also meet for an additional session to watch "Q&A with Editor" on DVD kit leader materials. Talk together about how you can make this more than a study you completed. How can you work together to equip yourselves and others to be effective apologists? How can you conduct periodic activities like those suggested in this process? You've made progress. Now both for yourself and your group, consider how you can make apologetics a vital lifestyle rather than simply a study.

• • • • •

ENDNOTES

Week One

1. Adapted from Bill Maher, *The View,* ABC, September 30, 2008.

2. Kate Rowinski, ed., *The Quotable Mom* (Guilford, CT: The Lyons Press, 2003), 295.

3. Gary Habermas, *Dealing with Doubt* (Chicago: Moody Press, 1990). Available from the Internet: *www.garyhabermas.com*

4. Paul E. Little, *Know Why You Believe* (Downers Grove, IL: InterVarsity Press, 2000), 19.

5. Ibid.

6. J. Gresham Machen, *What Is Faith?* (Carlisle, PA: The Banner of Truth Trust, 1991), 203.

7. Charles Colson, *How Now Shall We Live?* (Nashville: LifeWay Press, 1999), 12.

8. Neil T. Anderson, *Victory Over the Darkness* (Ventura, CA: Regal Books, 1990), 124.

9. "Argue," *Merriam-Webster Online Dictionary,* Merriam-Webster, Inc., [online, cited 8 July 2012]. Available from the Internet: *www.merriam-webster.com*

10. D.A. Carson, *The New Bible Commentary* (Downers Grove, IL: InterVarsity Press, 1994), Logos Bible Software.

11. "Dialegomai," *Thayer's Greek Lexicon* [online, cited 11 July 2012]. Available from the Internet: *concordances.org*

12. "Argue," *Merriam-Webster Online Thesaurus,* Merriam-Webster, Inc., [online, cited 11 July 2012]. Available from the Internet: *www.merriam-webster.com*

13. Gregory Koukl, *Tactics* (Grand Rapids, MI: Zondervan, 2009), 36.

14. C.S. Lewis, *Mere Christianity* (New York: Touchstone, 1996), 125.

15. *The Complete Works of Francis A. Schaeffer,* vol. 4, *A Christian View of the Church,* 2nd ed. (Wheaton, IL: Crossway, 1982), 189.

Week Two

1. "Oikia," *Strong's Concordance* [online, cited 11 July 2012]. Available from the Internet: *concordances.org*

2. Paul Copan, *True for You, But Not For Me* (Minneapolis: Bethany House, 1998), 35.

3. Adapted from "Tolerance," *Oxford Dictionaries,* Oxford University Press [online], April 2010 [cited 11 July 2012]. Available from the Internet: *www.oxforddictionaries.com*

4. Oprah Winfrey, *"A New Earth* Online Class," Oprah's Book Club Collection [online], 11 July 2008 [cited 9 July 2012]. Available from the Internet: *www.oprah.com*

5. Eckhart Tolle, *A New Earth* (New York: Penguin Group, 2005), 71. Available from the Internet: *www.amazon.com*

6. Ravi Zacharias, *Jesus Among Other Gods* (Nashville: Thomas Nelson, 2000), 7.

7. G.K. Chesterton, *Orthodoxy* (San Francisco: Ignatius Press, 1995), 135.

8. Ibid., 137.

9. Copan, *True for You,* 19.

10. Gary Habermas and Michael Licona, *The Case for the Resurrection of Jesus* (Grand Rapids, MI: Kregel, 2004).

11. Carson, *The New Bible Commentary,* Logos Bible Software.

12. Timothy Keller, *The Reason for God* (New York: Dutton, 2008), 202.

13. Doug Powell, *Holman QuickSource Guide to Christian Apologetics* (Nashville: Holman Reference, 2006), 267.

14. Craig Hazen, "Defending the Defense of the Faith," in *To Everyone An Answer,* eds. Francis Beckwith, William Lane Craig, and J.P. Moreland (Downers Grove, IL: InterVarsity Press, 2004), 39.

15. John F. Walvoord, Roy B. Zuck, and Dallas Theological Seminary, *The Bible Knowledge Commentary,* Logos Bible Software.

16. Little, *Know Why You Believe,* 15.

17. J.P. Moreland, *Love Your God with All Your Mind* (Colorado Springs: NavPress, 1997), 39.

18. Bart Ehrman, *Misquoting Jesus* (San Francisco: HarperCollins, 2005), 10.

19. J. Ed Komoszewski, M. James Sawyer, and Daniel B. Wallace, *Reinventing Jesus* (Grand Rapids, MI: Kregel, 2006), 76.

20. Ibid., 70–71.

21. Ibid., 71.

22. Clay Jones, "The Bibliographical Test Revisited" (presentation, Evangelical Theological Society, San Francisco, CA, November 16, 2011).

Week Three

1. Dietrich Bonhoeffer, *Life Together* (Minneapolis: Fortress Press, 2005), 98.

2. Nathaniel Bluedorn and Hans Bluedorn, *The Fallacy Detective* (Muscatine, IA: Christian Logic, 2003), 69.

3. Dallas Willard, *Renovation of the Heart* (Colorado Springs: NavPress, 2002), 124.

4. Ibid., 117.

5. Koukl, *Tactics,* 160–61.

"Errors in Reasoning" article (pp. 64–65)

1. "Informal Logic" *The Stanford Encyclopedia of Philosophy* [online], 28 November 2011 [cited 23 August 2012]. Available from: *http://plato.stanford.edu*

2. Adapted from M. Neil Browne and Stuart M. Keeley, *Asking the Right Questions* (Upper Saddle River, NJ: Pearson Education, Inc., 2007), 84.

3. Adapted from Bluedorn and Bluedorn, *The Fallacy Detective*, 53.

4. Ibid., 51.

5. Peter Kreeft, *Socratic Logic* (South Bend, IN: St. Augustine Press, 2010), 80.

6. Ibid., 81.

7. Ibid., 82.

8. Bluedorn and Bluedorn, *The Fallacy Detective*, 71.

9. Bluedorn and Bluedorn, *The Fallacy Detective*, 38.

10. Browne and Keeley, *Asking the Right Questions,* 95.

11. Bluedorn and Bluedorn, *The Fallacy Detective*, 41.

12. Ibid.

Week Four

1. Warren Wiersbe, *The Bible Expository Commentary* (Wheaton, IL: Victor Books, 1996), Logos Bible Software.

2. Sue Bolin, "Four Killer Questions," Probe Ministries [online, cited 8 July 2012]. Available from the Internet: *www.probe.org*

3. Norman L. Geisler and Frank Turek, *I Don't Have Enough Faith to Be an Atheist* (Wheaton, IL: Crossway Books, 2004), 39.

4. Wiersbe, *The Bible Expository Commentary,* Logos Bible Software.

5. For further reading see Robert Bowman and J. Ed Komoszweski, *Putting Jesus in His Place* (Grand Rapids, MI: Kregel, 2007).

6. Saint Augustine, *Confessions* (New York: Oxford, 1991), 2000.

7. "Theodore Roosevelt Quotes," *Brainy Quotes* [online, cited 24 July 2012]. Available from the Internet: *www.brainyquote.com*

8. Pudd'nhead Wilson's New Calendar quoted in Mark Twain, *Following the Equator* (New York: Harper & Brothers Publishers, 1906), 132. Available from the Internet: *http://books.google.com*

9. William Lane Craig, "In Intellectual Neutral," Reasonable Faith [online, cited 8 July 2012]. Available from the Internet: *www.reasonablefaith.org*

10. Kenneth Daniels, *Why I Believed* (Duncanville, TX: Kenneth W. Daniels, 2009), 66.

11. Plato, *The Trial and Death of Socrates* (Indianapolis, IN: Hackett Publishing Co., Inc., 2000), 39.

12. Bluedorn and Bluedorn, *The Fallacy Detective*, 108.

13. Adapted from Koukl, *Tactics,* 84–85.

14. Richard Dawkins, *River Out of Eden* (New York: Basic Books, 1995), 133.

15. Christopher Hitchens, *God is Not Great* (New York: Twelve, 2007), 102.

16. Ibid., 282.

17. Sam Harris, *The End of Faith* (W.W. Norton & Company, Inc., 2004), 173.

18. Adapted from Richard Dawkins, *The God Delusion* (New York: Mariner Books, 2008), 77.

19. This phrase is commonly used by Muslims.

20. Ernest Hemingway, *A Farewell to Arms* (Toronto: Harper Perennial Classics, 2012), 8.

Week Five

1. C.S. Lewis, *The Problem of Pain* (San Francisco: HarperCollins, 2001), 48.

2. Dan Kimball, *They Like Jesus But Not the Church* (Grand Rapids, MI: Zondervan, 2007).

3. G.K. Chesterton, *What's Wrong With the World?* [online, cited 9 July 2012]. Available from the Internet: *www.gutenberg.org*

4. Luke Muehlhauser, "About Me," Common Sense Atheism [online, cited 12 July 2012]. Available from the Internet: *http://commonsenseatheism.com*

5. Chesterton, *Orthodoxy*, 38.

6. "Dignity," *Merriam-Webster Online Dictionary*, Merriam-Webster, Inc., [online, cited 12 July 2012]. Available from the Internet: *www.merriam-webster.com*

7. Robert B. Hughes and J. Carl Laney, *Tyndale Bible Commentary* (Wheaton, IL: Tyndale House Publishers, 1990), Logos Bible Software.

8. Ibid.

9. Koukl, *Tactics*.

10. Copan, *True for You*, 39.

11. Adapted from Moreland, *Love Your God*, 147.

12. Ibid., 145.

13. Philip Ginsbury and Raphael Culter, *The Phases of Jewish History* (Israel: Devora Publishing Company, 2005), 268. Available from the Internet: *http://books.google.com*

Week Six

1. "About the Foundation," Freedom From Religion Foundation [online, cited 24 July 2012]. Available from the Internet: *www.ffrf.org*

2. Chesterton, *Orthodoxy*, 29.

3. "Top Ad Campaigns of the 20th Century," CNBC [online, cited 13 June 2012]. Available from the Internet: *www.cnbc.com*

4. Adapted from Randy Newman, *Questioning Evangelism* (Grand Rapids, MI: Zondervan, 2004), 28.

5. Moreland, *Love Your God*, 135.

6. "Six Reasons Young Christians Leave the Church," Barna Group [online], 28 September 2011 [cited 14 August 2012]. Available from the Internet: *www.barna.org*

7. *Complete Works of Francis A. Schaeffer*, vol. 4, *A Christian View of the Church*, 181.